STEP-BY-STEP

Pa

Windows

STEP-BY-STEP

Paradox for Windows

P.K.McBride

Newtech
An Imprint of Butterworth-Heinemann Ltd
Linacre House, Jordan Hill, Oxford OX2 8DP

R| A member of the Reed Elsevier group

OXFORD   LONDON   BOSTON
MUNICH   NEW DELHI SINGAPORE SYDNEY
TOKYO   TORONTO   WELLINGTON

First published 1993
© P.K.McBride 1993

All rights reserved. No part of this publication may be reproduced in any material form (including photocopying or storing in any medium by electronic means and whether or not transiently or incidentally to some other use of this publication) without the written permission of the copyright holder except in accordance with the provisions of the Copyright, Design and Patents Act 1988 or under the terms of a licence issued by the Copyright Licensing Agency Ltd, 90 Tottenham Court Road, London England W1P 9HE. Applications for the copyright holder's written permission to reproduce any part of this publication should be addressed to the publishers.

NOTICE
The author and the publisher have used their best efforts to prepare this book, including the computer examples contained in it. The computer examples have all been tested. The author and the publisher make no warranty, implicit or explicit, about the documentation. The author and the publisher will not be liable under any circumstances for any direct or indirect damages arising from any use, direct or indirect, of the documentation or computer examples contained in this book.

TRADEMARKS/REGISTERED TRADEMARKS
Computer hardware and software brand names mentioned in this book are protected by their respective trademarks and are acknowledged.

British Library Cataloguing in Publication Data
A catalogue record for this book is available from the British Library.

ISBN 0 7506 0610 X

Typeset by the author
Printed and bound in Great Britain

Contents

Introduction 9

-1- Data Basics

1	Data and Information 14
2	Files and Fields 16
3	Field Types 20
4	Paradox and Windows 23
5	The Desktop 26
6	Paradox Objects 30
7	Aliases and Directories 36

- 2 - Working with Single Tables

8	Creating a Database 42
9	Defining a New Table 47
10	Saving and Opening Files 52
11	Adding and Editing Records 56
12	Altering the Table Layout 63
13	Using Forms 65
14	Designing a Form 68
15	Properties and Design 74
16	Searching 79
17	Queries on a Single Table 82
18	Simple Record Selection 86

Contents

19	Selection with Multiple Criteria	90
20	The Answer Table	95
21	Sorting into Order	98

-3- Outputs from the Database

22	Reporting Out	104
23	Report Design	108
24	The Report Design Window	111
25	Bands in Reports	113
26	Report Design - Text	118
27	Mailing Labels	122
28	Combined Fields	127
29	The Project Folder	130

- 4 - Relational Databases

30	A Stock Control System	134
31	Friendlier Forms	136
32	Query by Example	139
33	Queries in Linked Tables	141
34	Calculations in Queries	144
35	Renaming Answer Fields	147
36	Calculations in Reports	149
37	Catalogues from Files	152

Contents

- 5 - Graphical Displays

38	Graphic Objects	158
39	OLE Objects	163
40	Crosstabs	165
41	Two-Field Crosstabs	170
42	Graphs	171
43	Multiple Series Graphs	174
44	Alternative Graph Types	178

- 6 - Methods

45	Automated Systems	186
46	Scripts and Methods	188
47	Buttons	190
48	Conditional Actions	195
49	Variables	198
50	Handling Files in Methods	201
51	Menus in Methods	205
52	Handling Menu Selections	209
53	Automated Stock Control	213
54	Custom Methods	218

Index 225

Introduction

The problem in writing about Paradox for Windows is deciding where to start. Here is a massive system - over 12 Megabytes of disk space - with tremendous potential and enormous flexibility. This is a database that takes full advantage of all that Windows has to offer. Amongst other things, that means easy file access, multiple file displays, attractive screens, intuitive working, and - mustn't forget this - databases that can handle pictures as well as the usual types of data. And there's more to it than that. Paradox for Windows is more than a database. It's graph-maker, report-writer and desktop publisher.

So where to start? I didn't see much point in working through the system explaining each command and feature. The manuals and the on-line help pages do that very thoroughly. They will tell you what each does and how they work. This information will be invaluable as you extend your expertise, but I believe that when you come to any new system - especially one as fully-featured as Paradox - what you need most is an idea of how it all fits together in practice. If you have been right through the process of setting up and using a database once, then you can do it again with other sets of data. This book is designed with this in mind.

The first section sets the background. There's an initial chapter, mainly for users new to databases, that covers the main concepts, potential uses and the jargon. We'll then take a look at Paradox for Windows to see what it can do - as a straight database management system and beyond. The remainder of the book demonstrates Paradox in practice. We'll start with the simpler 'flat-file' databases - single file systems. Amongst the examples there is a client file for an estate agents, and a simple stock-control system. You will see how to get data into them and meaningful information out of them.

9

Introduction

We then move on to develop a relational database system - one that draws data from several different files. The example builds on the earlier client file, adding a list of properties and of agents, and you will see how the three can be cross-linked freely. In the final sections, we'll be delving deeper into Paradox, exploring graphing and graphic objects, and taking a look at its programming capabilities.

Work through the examples as you read - perhaps changing the data to suit your own interests and experience.

Like most other modern software packages, Paradox for Windows offers a number of different ways to call up each of its many commands and facilities. You will often find that you can accomplish the same end by clicking an icon, selecting from menus with either the mouse or key letters, pressing a function key or pressing a [Control] key combination. Some of the alternatives are designed for existing Paradox for DOS users, so that they can carry their skills directly across. Some are there to make life simpler or faster. Such a multiplicity of methods does not, however, make life simpler for the writer, and can be confusing to the new user. I don't think that you really want to wade through a list of alternative approaches each time we come to something new, so I will normally give only one way of carrying out any operation, and that will normally be with the mouse and the menus. It's the way I prefer to work all the time, but if you want to trim a few seconds off each job, the keyboard shortcuts, are all given in the User's Guide.

Paradox for Windows can be run a 386-based PC with 4 MB of main memory, 15 Mb of free space on the hard disk, an EGA screen and Windows 3.0 or later. This is very much the bare minimum. While writing this book, I have been running Paradox under Windows 3.1 on a DAN Technology 486DX/33 with 8Mb of main memory and

Introduction

a Trident VGA display. That has given me a consistently clear display and good performance. Paradox is large and complex, and slows down somewhat where there are graphics in the data files, screen displays or reports, and when it is running methods - programs written in Paradox's own language. I would not want to run this software on a 386SX machine, though I suspect that is true of many of the new Windows applications.

It doesn't take much to get Paradox up and running - the supplied installation program does a smooth, efficient job. It will create an appropriate directory structure, set up the Windows application and adjust the start-of-day routines. It requires very little from you, apart from changing the disks. After the main installation is complete, you should edit your CONFIG.SYS file to set the files and buffers. The relevant lines should read:

FILES = 60
BUFFERS = 40   (10 is enough if you have a disk cache)

That FILES figure controls the number of files that you can have open at once, and might have to be increased. During a typical Paradox session, you will open a number of data files, and Paradox will open a lot more, for temporary data storage and for its own purposes. Your other Windows applications will also have files open. Borland recommend FILES = 60. Running Paradox alongside a word-processing, graphics and DTP software, I have found that the system crashes occasionally at this number. With FILES increased to 64, I have had no problems. If you do hit trouble running Paradox, try resetting FILES to a higher value.

There is also a separate Configuration Utility that network users will have to run through before using Paradox.

Introduction

As Paradox is Windows-based and as it is consistent in its approach in all its aspects, it is quick and easy to learn - up to a point. It doesn't take long to master the basics, and the basics are all you need for a great deal of routine business data management. Learning to create fully-fledged applications takes longer, but even then Paradox is still significantly simpler and quicker to use than comparable DOS-based data managment systems - and it is not an all-or-nothing matter. You can build up from basics, adding on extra features, linking tables, forms and queries, as and when you are ready. I hope that this book will help to ease you through the basics and on to get the best out of Paradox for Windows.

P.K.McBride
Southampton
Spring 1993

- 1 -
Data Basics

1 Data and Information

In ordinary usage, **data** and **information** have the same meaning, but in computing the two are significantly different. **Data** is the raw material, a mass of facts and figures. **Information** is data that has been processed into a meaningful pattern - though just because you have processed data through a computer does not mean you will get information out of it. That's what should happen, but whether it does or not depends largely on how the data is stored and the kind of questions that you ask.

For example, a firm may have have computerised its stock data - details of prices, suppliers, stock levels, storage bays and the rest. If the managers then ask the computer to print out a full stock list, they will have more or less what they started with - lots of data. If they want the sort of information that will help them to manage effectively, they must ask questions like "Which items need re-stocking?", "Which lines are most profitable?", and "Where did we put the widgets?"

To get sensible answers, the data must have been stored originally in some sort of organised fashion. You don't need computers, of course, to organise data and to ask questions - computers just make it easier and quicker - and a good manual/paper system is better than a bad computerised one any day. So let's start with a quick look at traditional filing systems.

Probably the simplest and most familiar system is the address book. A well organised book will have its entries arranged alphabetically, or sorted by category, with each laid out to a fixed pattern and be kept up to date. You will be able to flick through quickly to find a person's name and read their address, (laid out neatly underneath), or their phone number, (from the column alongside). It's an important point that the data for each person is actually a collection

Data and Information 1

of separate items - name, street, town, postcode, phone number. Arranging them so that each is in its appointed place makes it easy to find any specific item of information.

To go back to the earlier example, a manual stock control system would probably have a card for each stock line. There will be many more items of data for each line - cost and sale prices, supplier code, bin number, re-order level, quantity in stock and all the rest. Layout is even more important here than with the address book, as there are so many more items of data. The store manager should be able to get the information he wants by glancing at the right place on the card. If the data has been jotted down haphazardly, it's going to be difficult to find later.

The professionals have a term for it GIGO - Garbage In, Garbage Out. If you are going to use a database successfully, you must be fairly clear from the start about what information you want from it, and how you can organise data to make that possible. Paradox does simplify the process. It recognises that your needs may change over time and that you may not get it right at the start. It therefore provides easy and safe ways to reorganise later. So, pre-planning helps, but don't panic!

2 Files and Fields

In computer terms, the data held on one person or one stock item is referred to as a **record**; individual data items within each record are **fields**. It may help, initially, to think of the record as a card in a card index system. (They'll get more complex later, but that's another matter.) The fields are then the lines or marked off boxes on the card. In a computer system, they may also be laid out on a card-style screen display, but each field will be identified by a name.

All the records in a set will have the same number of fields - though some may be left empty. Real world data doesn't always fall into nice neat categories. Look what happens when I try to organise my address book. Here are two typical entries:

Aunt Margie,
Rose Cottage,
Flowery End,
off Lily Lane,
Little Troubled,
nr Snugchester,
Sleepishire, SP3 4ZZ

Jim Short,
147a Greater Titchfield Street,
London, WC1A 1CW
071 234 5678
0831 123400 (Car)
071 234 7890 (Fax)

Aunt Margie's address runs to six lines, compared to Jim's two. Jim has phone, car phone and fax numbers while Aunt Margie remains firmly off-line. The size of the items also varies. In Aunt Margie's entry, the longest item has only 15 characters, but Jim's street line

Files and Fields 2

is twice as long. When I get round to transferring my address book onto the computer, I shall have to allow six fields, each of 30 characters, for the address and at least three for the telecom links.

Fields	Redcord 1	Record 2
Name:	Aunt Margie	Jim Short
Address1:	Rose Cottage	147a Greater Titchfield Street
Address2:	Flowery End	
Address3:	off Lily Lane	
Address4:	Little Troubled	
Town:	nr Snugchester	London
County:	Sleepishire	
Postcode:	SP3 4ZZ	WC1A 1CW
Tel:		071 234 5678
Carphone:		0831 123400
Fax:		071 234 7890

Finding a suitable field structure for your data can be something of a problem at times! We'll return to this later when we set up our first example database. Meanwhile, let's get back to defining some terms.

File

A **file** is a collection of records, all of the same type, stored as a unit in the computer system. The nearest equivalent in the traditional office is the card file or a summary sheet, rather than "file" in the sense of a card folder containing a set of loose pages.

As you will see when you get into Paradox, you can look at the file one record at a time - as with cards in a card file, or view a screenful at once in a table display. There, each record occupies a line (which may well extend off the visible screen), with the fields arranged down

17

2 Files and Fields

the columns. This view helps to emphasise the point that you can slice through a file in two ways. By taking a 'horizontal' slice, you can pull out all the data on one item. By slicing vertically you can make comparisons or get summary totals across the fields.

Part ref.	Description	Supplier	Cost	VAT	Quantity	Value
W123	Widget, large	AWM	3.07	1	26	79.82
W125	Widget, small	AWM	1.19	1	93	110.67
K534	Kitchen Gadget	GSC	16.58	1	14	232.12

You can see from this example that by searching down through the **Supplier** field, we could find all those items that come from AWM, or by totalling the **Value** fields we could get a full stock valuation.

Key Field

A **key field** is one used to keep the file in order. With an address book, if the Name was the key field, the records would automatically fall into alphabetical order by name. A key field is not essential. If there isn't one, the records will be stored in the order in which they were entered. In either case, you can sort the file at any time, arranging it by alphabetical or numeric order - ascending or descending - based on any of the fields.

Database

The term **database** is sometimes used to refer to a software package such as Paradox. This is not correct. Paradox, dBase and their ilk are **database management systems**. A database is the body of data managed by such software. The simplest type is a **flat-file database** - one that consists of a single file. It might be a firm's stock records, a club's membership list or your own address book. If you wanted to perform only basic sorting, searching and list or label printing on

Files and Fields   2

a single file, then **Cardfile**, one of the Windows Accessories, would have all facilities that you needed. Paradox can be used for such limited aims - very successfully - but it will also do much more. Flat-file management is, however, the place to start, and we'll do that when we've finished painting in the background.

A **relational database** is one that consists of a set of related files. Each will be physically separate on the disk and could be accessed independently as a flat-file, but they will have one or more fields in common, creating links between them.

You might, for example, have a file of stock details and a second containing the suppliers' addresses, with the two linked by a reference number or code. When you run a check to see which items need reordering, the list that you produce will have the stock lines and the necessary supplier details. The beauty of it is that it's all done in one operation. If the stock and suppliers files were managed separately, you would have to first look up the low lines, then go through the suppliers' file to get the addresses. The alternative single-file approach would have the full invoicing details of the supplier in each stock line - creating a horrendous update job whenever the details change!

In a fully integrated business, a database might cover stock, equipment, suppliers, customers, personnel, and the rest. By making full use of the links between them, you can create a system in which entering a sale will update the stock records, generate an invoice, add the bill to the client's account and credit the sales staff with their commissions. This book won't quite take you to that level, but I hope it will give you sufficient grasp of the essentials and the confidence to explore and experiment further.

19

3   Field Types

What kind of data can you store in a database? The answer, with Paradox, is "more or less anything - as long as you tell it what to expect." Paradox can handle 10 different types of data, each of which is stored in its own special format. Exactly how it stores the data is largely irrelevant to us - all we need to know is the types so that we can decide which type is best for which field.

Paradox for Windows can manage files in four different formats - more if you have other database drivers on your system. The four supplied formats are Paradox for Windows (of course), Paradox 3.5, dBase IV and dBase III+. Each has its own distinct set of data types. The standard Paradox set is more extensive and makes better use of the facilities available under Windows. The other sets can be ignored unless you want to take existing files and manage them with Paradox for Windows, or you want to be able to link your new files with those managed by the other systems.

Paradox Field Types

Alphanumeric
This is for any kind of characters - letters, digits and symbols. Names and addresses and the like are obviously alphanumeric - but so are some kinds of numbers. Telephone numbers, for instance, must be treated as characters not numbers, otherwise an entry such as "071 123 4567" would be stored - and displayed - as 711234567.

Short Numbers
These can only hold whole numbers in between -32,768 and +32,767. These take up less memory and disk space than ordinary numbers, though in these days of cheap mass storage, that is less of a consideration than it used to be.

Field Types 3

Number
This will hold any kind of number - the maximum size is astronomical and not to be worried about, though there is a limit to the accuracy. Paradox only stores the first 12 digits accurately. In financial terms this means that once you get over 1,000 billion pounds, it starts to forget about the pennies. Numbers are normally displayed in full, but once beyond the accuracy limit are displayed in Scientific format. Try to write in 123,456,789,012.34 and it will appear as 1.23456789012e11. That works out to:

1.23456789012 x 10 to the power of 11
= 1.23456789012 x 100,000,000,000
= 123,456,789,012.0.

You have lost the 34p, but I doubt that it will be missed!

$ - Currency
a special number format for money. Values will be displayed with two places of decimals and a pound sign at the front. The 12 digit accuracy limit applies here as well.

Date
These store dates in the form **DD/MM/YY**. There's some flexibility about how you enter them. **"5/4/93"**, **"5-4-93"**, **"5 4 93"**, **"5th April 1993"** - all of these would be accepted and converted to **"05/04/93"**.

You could use an Alphanumeric field to store a date, but you would lose out. With a proper Date field, values are checked as they are entered, to make sure they are valid dates, and you can later sort records into date order or search for those that are before, after or on any given date.

3 Field Types

Memo
These act as notes attached to records. They are stored in an unusual way, partly inside but mainly outside the normal file structure. This makes them unlimited in size. You can specify that anything from 1 to 240 characters should be stored in the record - and this part is then visible on screen in the normal display. Should any of your memo fields contain more than the set minimum, then the overflow will be stored in a separate file.

Formatted Memo
As far as data storage goes, these are the same as ordinary memos, but style and layout formats can be imposed on them.

Graphic
Use these for photos, diagrams and screen shots. These can be imported from a file or pasted into via the Windows Clipboard. Storage space could well be a consideration here, as even a relatively small and simple image could take 40 Kb or more.

OLE
Object Linking and Embedding exploits Window's ability to create dynamic links between applications. If a picture is pasted from another program into an OLE field rather than as a straight Graphic, the Paradox image will be updated automatically if it is edited in the originating program.

Binary
These are a special case. They can only be used from ObjectPAL, and not directly from Paradox.

Fields of these last five types are sometimes referred to as **BLOB**s - Binary Large OBjects. Look out for them later.

Paradox and Windows   4

Paradox for Windows is designed as an intuitive system - and as they say, that's all right if you know how to intuit. If you are already using other Windows application, you should have no trouble in handling all the 'tools'. (Producing something useful with them is a different matter, of course.) If you are completely new to Windows, could I suggest that you spend an hour or two exploring that system before you turn to Paradox. Play the games, draw some pictures with Paintbrush, root around the directories with the File Manager and dip into the Help pages wherever you go. You don't need to become an expert, but you should at least learn these basic techniques.

■ Control the Mouse

Click the left button to locate the cursor, select options or highlight items.

Double-click (press twice rapidly) to load files, and sometimes to select operations. If a single click doesn't do it, try a double.

Click right is less common. In Paradox, right clicking an icon or other screen object will call up a menu which controls its appearance or other optional features.

Drag - hold down the left button and move the mouse - to move things around the screen, highlight areas or draw boxes.

■ Select from Menus

Only those options that are applicable at the time are shown in bold. Move the highlight bar to an option either by dragging it, or by pointing and clicking. To leave without making a selection, press [Escape] or point and click elsewhere on the screen.

4 Paradox and Windows

The option names may be accompanied by:

a **tick**, showing that this is a toggle (on/off) option, and is on;

an **arrowhead**, meaning that a sub-menu will open if you highlight this option;

a **keystroke shortcut**, e.g. **Shift-F8**, which you can use as an alternative to the menu system.

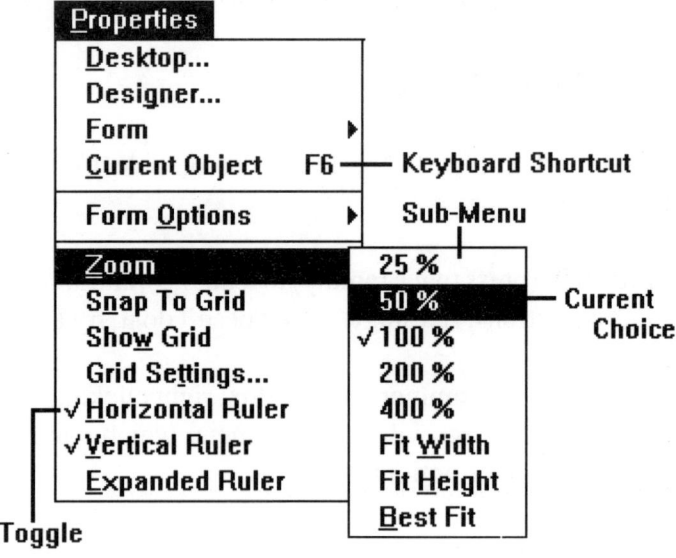

■ Use the Window Frame

Move the window by dragging on the top bar.

Resize it by dragging on the right edge, bottom or bottom right corner of the frame.

Paradox and Windows 4

Scroll the view through the window using the scroll bar - either by clicking the arrows or dragging the slider.

Call up the **Control Menu** by clicking the top left button.

Close a window by double clicking the top left button.

Click the **Maximize** button to switch to full screen, then shrink it with the double-headed arrow button that replaces it.

Click the **Minimize** button to reduce the window to an icon.

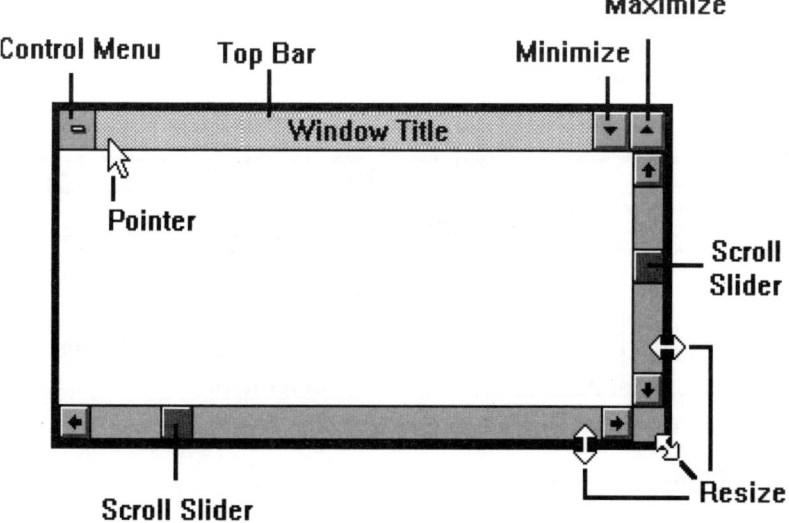

■ Recognise Icons

In Paradox, these can represent files and design tools - as in other Windows applications, but they are also there as a quick way to call up some of the more frequently used operations.

Time to go hands-on - if you have not already dipped into Paradox. Load it up and explore the screen as you read the next section.

25

5 The Desktop

At first sight the Paradox opening screen can be rather daunting - I think it's a combination of that clear white background and the cryptic words and odd little icons along the top. They call this screen the **Desktop**, and that's the way to think about it. The main area is your working space, and the menu words and icons are your tools, all neatly laid out ready for a work session. This is where you will spread your files, forms and other "papers" when you get busy. You will be able to slide them around, fold them up small and push them to the side if you want them out of the way for a while, and pull the one you are most interested in, to the top of the pile.

Let's see what tools we have to work with.

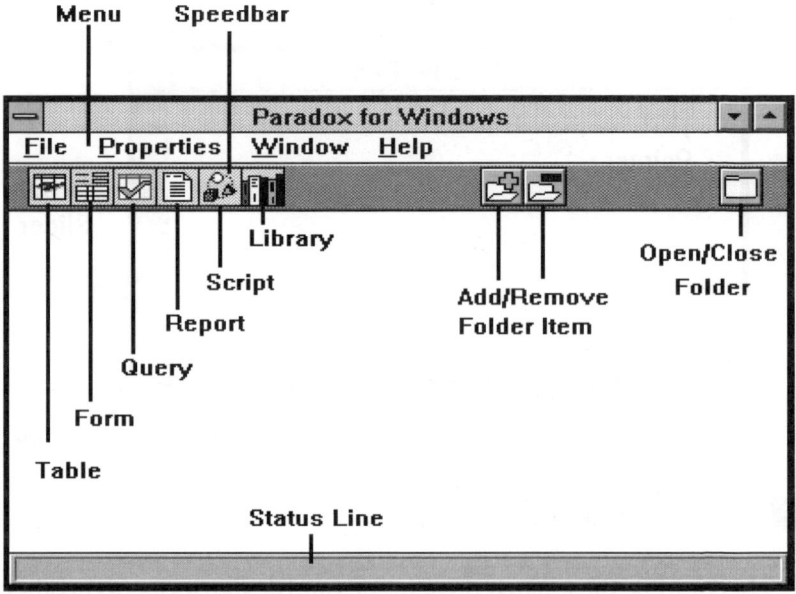

The very top line is part of the Window frame and has the usual control buttons. You may find it useful to click the Maximize button at the start of a session to give yourself plenty of working space.

26

The Desktop 5

The second line is the **Menu Bar**. Initially there are four menus on offer. These will always be present, but others will also appear here later according to the type of file that you are working on at the time.

The Desktop Menu Bar

The **File** menu is essentially for setting up new files or opening existing ones. There are also a set of Utilities, for copying, renaming and moving data between files; a Printer Setup routine, which we'll leave until we have something to print; Multiuser (network) control and information; System Settings, which can be ignored for the time being, Aliases and the Directories are also managed from here (see Section 7); and finally there is the Exit.

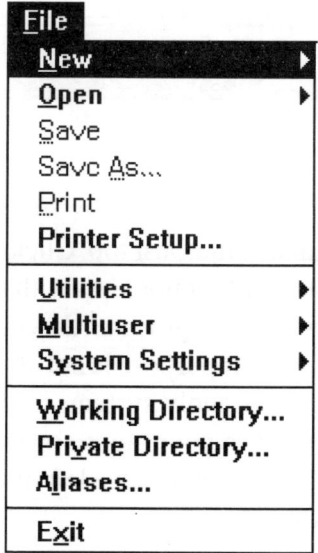

The **Properties** menu is at this stage only concerned with the appearance of the Desktop itself. You may like to use this to change

27

| **5** | **The Desktop** |

the background - your own BMP images or any of the Windows background BMP files can be used. I like things the way they are, but tastes differ.

You will find that when you have loaded a table, form or report, this menu gives you control of its screen appearance.

The **Window** menu relates to windows opened within Paradox - not the main Desktop window. When you have several files open at once - each in its own window - this will let you arrange them in tile or cascade form.

Help is always available and organised in the standard Windows way.

The Speed Bar

This occupies the third line of the Desktop. Clicking on these icons gives you quick access to key functions. As with the Menu Bar, the contents of the speed bar will change to suit the current activity. The icons are rather small and their purpose is not always immediately obvious. But this is a user-friendly system, so there's no need to struggle to identify them. Run your mouse over these icons now. You will see that their labels pop into the left of the **Status Bar** at the bottom of the Desktop.

The five icons on the left of the Speedbar offer quick ways of setting up new files of different types - Table, Form, Query, Report and Script. We'll get back to these in the next few chapters. The Open

The Desktop 5

Library icon is a convenience for ObjectPAL programmers, and of litle interest to us at this level. The remaining icons relate to Folders. A **Folder** is a set of files, kept together for easy access. We'll get back to those later.

The Status Bar

This line, at the bottom of the Desktop, helps you to keep track of what you are doing. Its contents vary according to the type of work that you are doing at the time. We've already noted that it displays a reminder of the purpose of an icon, whenever the cursor points to one. When you are working on a file, it will also tell you the number of the current record and how many there are in the file, and prompts will pop up here when you make some types of errors.

6 Paradox Objects

In Paradox, the data files, documents and other items that you can create or manipulate are all referred to as **objects**. Though varied in nature, they have many features in common - key ones being that you can store an object on disk and represent it on screen as a window or icon. The **major objects** are Tables, Forms, Reports, Queries and Scripts.

A second set of **design objects** exploit the Paradox/Windows graphic potential. They include graphs, that can be drawn from your data files, and means of including pictures within records, as well as a number of ways of enhancing reports and other documents.

All objects have **properties** and **methods**. The major objects and most of the design objects also have other, subsidiary, objects within them - the columns in tables, labels on forms, any data fields anywhere - which also have their own properties and methods.

The properties relate mainly to screen appearance - the typeface, size and colour of the text that appears in the object; the width of columns in tables; the background colour of a form. These properties can be changed as often as you like, whenever you like, and without affecting the data itself. To change the properties of an object, simply point to it and click on the right mouse button. A menu will open, showing you what can be changed.

An object's methods govern how the object behaves. Most of these are fixed by the system, for obvious reasons, and the rest are probably best left to advanced users.

We'll come back to all of these later, but for the moment, let's concentrate on the essentials.

Paradox Objects 6

Tables

The most important object in the Paradox system is the **table** - the data file. The choice of name helps to emphasise how you would normally view it - as a table with the records on the rows and the columns dividing them into fields.

A table is created by defining the field structure. You would do this by telling Paradox how many fields there are, what each is to be called and what type of data they will contain. You do not have to - indeed you cannot - specify the number of records it will have. The table will hold as many records as you have entered - one at first, hundreds or thousands when you have finished. Paradox does set limits, but they are so high that most of us can cheerfully ignore them. In theory it can cope with up to 2 billion records, or a total of 260 million characters. Most of us will run out of hard disk space or customers long before this!

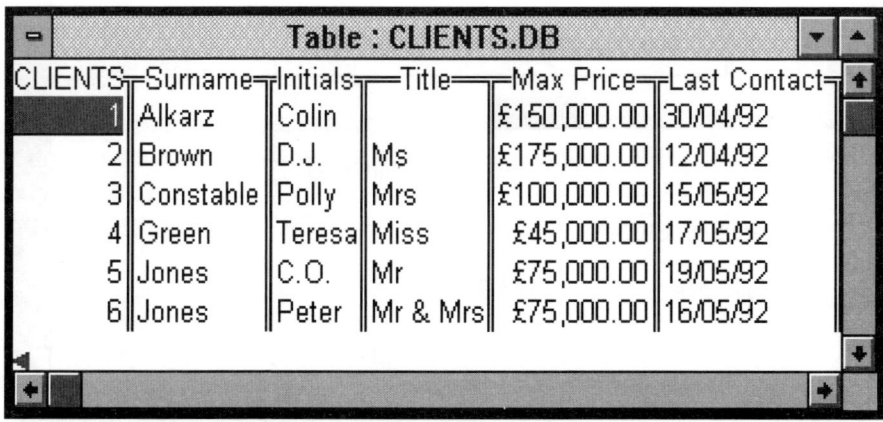

The table view is compact and allows easy comparison of the same fields in different records. The problem with it is that records will usually have more fields than will fit across the screen. You can scroll

31

6   Paradox Objects

it left or right to see the missing ones, but there are times when it is useful to have the whole of one record displayed on screen. For this you need a **form**.

Forms

Paradox will create a form for you at the touch of an icon, giving a simple layout with the fields arranged in lines down the screen. If you prefer, you can design the form yourself. You might do this to bring the more important or more frequently updated fields closer together. If there are so many fields that they disappear off the bottom of the screen, then repositioning them to bring them all into view would be a good idea. When designing the form, you can add text, to make things clearer for the data entry clerk, and lines, boxes or other graphics to improve readability and the general appearance.

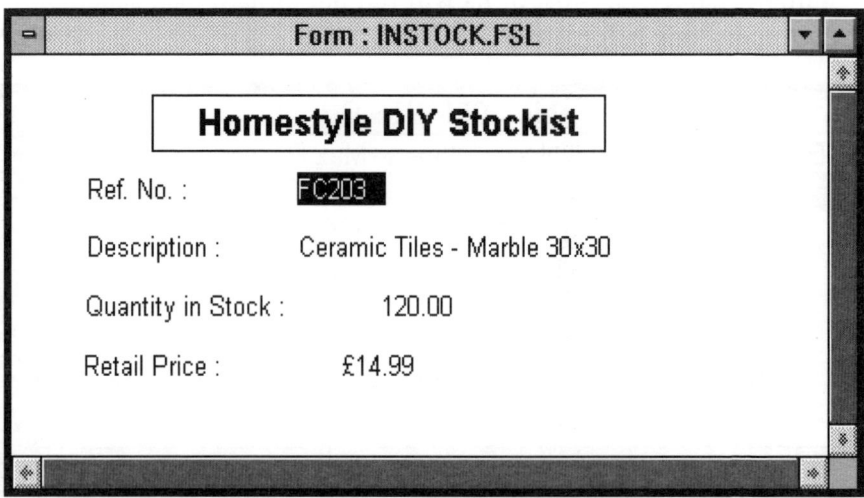

A form does not have to include all the fields. Some may be removed from the display, either for security purposes or because they are not relevant to the job in hand. As any one table can have several forms

Paradox Objects 6

associated with it, this is worth bearing in mind. On a stock control system, for example, you might have three forms. One would be for use at the front desk, where cutomers could see it, and would display only the description, retail price and quantity in stock. A second, designed for the storeshand would show reference numbers and storage locations. The third would carry the fuller details needed by the stores manager.

Reports

The third major object is a **report**. This defines the appearance and the contents of a print out from a table. Forms and reports can be used interchangeably - the main difference is that a form is designed primarily for the screen, while a report is really meant for printer output.

03 February 1993   STOCK   Page 1

Ref	Description	Cost	Qty	Reord	Retail
FC203	Ceramic Tiles - Marble 30x30	£9.23	120	50	£14.99
FC214	Ceramic Tiles - Grey 30x30	£8.79	60	50	£14.99
FW501	Hardwood Flooring - Ash	£17.45	20	10	£23.99
FW502	Hardwood Flooring - Beech	£17.45	8	10	£23.99
WP309	Wallpaper - Woodchip - 11 yd	£0.95	72	100	£1.49
WP313	Wallpaper - Embossed - 18yd	£1.45	40	30	£2.25
WT207	Tiles - Grey/Floral 11x11cm	£13.26	40	25	£16.99
WT411	Tiles - Black Diamond 20x20cm	£15.85	15	25	£18.49
WW709	Cladding, T & G - 1800x10cm	£4.89	24	20	£6.99
WW712	Shiplap Cladding - 1800x10cm	£4.05	8	10	£5.99

6   Paradox Objects

The records can be sorted and grouped by categories, and you can select which fields to include, and where to place them. Headings, page numbers and other text can be added freely. As with forms, you can have several reports linked to one file. That stock control system might produce a customer catalogue, full stock valuation and re-order list. This last, of course, will not - or should not in a well-organised business - include all stock items. Now a report will always include all the records in a table, but the table that you send to the report can be a sub-set of your main data file. Which brings us nicely to the next object.

Queries

A **query** is used to select a group of records from a table. The query defines what you are looking for, and which fields you want to include in the output list. On screen, it appears as a simple table, into which the specifications are written, and it can be saved as a file, for future use.

Suppose that one of your suppliers goes out of business. You need to know all the stock lines that had been sourced from there so that you can organise alternative supplies. The query on your stock table would specify the old supplier's reference and include the parts' codes, descriptions and prices.

A query can check and draw data from several tables at once. When reordering stock, you might want to know what items need replacing (from your stock table) and how much credit you still have with the relevant suppliers (from your accounts table). The resulting list will then tell you what should be ordered and how much cash you will have to find to get the orders filled. (I'm assuming - no doubt wrongly - that you have the same cashflow problems as I do.)

Paradox Objects 6

The output from the query takes the form of a new table, containing *copies* of your data - the original table is untouched. The new table, called ANSWER, is created automatically by Paradox. It has only a temporary existence. It will be overwritten by the next query, and scrapped at the end of the working session. In most cases, you would pass it straight on to a report for printing or you might give it a new (permanent) name if you wanted to save it for later reference.

Scripts

The last of the major objects is the **script**. Scripts are used to automate routine chores. They are sets of instructions written in ObjectPAL (Paradox's Progammable Application Language). They are the free-standing equivalent of **methods**, which are generally shorter and are attached to forms. If you are a non-programmer, the idea may seem a little daunting at first, but don't be put off. Scripts and methods don't have to be long and complex to be useful. You will find that there are a number of tasks that you have to do regularly and always in the same way. If you can set up script for these, you can reduce each to a single button press instead of a sequence of operations. It saves time, reduces the chances of error and simplifies the whole process so that you can hand the job over to a less skilled person. It doesn't take long to learn all you need to create such limited purpose scripts.

7   Aliases and Directories

An **alias** is a short and convenient alternative a full directory path name. It would allow you, for example, to type "ACCS92" instead of "C:\PDOXWIN\MAINDATA\ACCOUNTS\YR92_93". Selecting the alias then gets you to the right directory. It saves typing and it's easier to remember than a full directory path.

This may not seem that important when you can select directories and files by clicking icons or names in a list. However, it is a different matter when you start to write scripts. There you will have to type the names and directories. And an alias won't just save you a little typing when you have to give a directory path - it will save it every time you have to give the path. It means that you can develop an application with the test files in a temporary directory. When you want to put it to real use, you won't need to hunt through the script rewriting paths. All you will have to do is reassign the alias to the proper directory. But that's for later. There are some aliases that are relevant to all of us, and they might need some attention now.

Paradox has two built-in aliases that you may need to change before you do anything. WORK identifies your normal working directory; PRIV is mainly relevant to network users - it stands for your private directory. The installation process sets up directories called 'WORKING' and 'PRIVATE', and links those aliases to them.

If you are working on a stand-alone PC, not a network, and are still experimenting with the software, then you can simply leave the settings as they are. Later, when you have start to create database files and want them properly organised into their own directories, you will have to come back to this. If you are a network user, then aliases and directories should be sorted out now.

Aliases and Directories   7

The Working Directory

When you try to load a file, if you don't specify a path, Paradox will look in your **working directory**, wherever that may be. Set it up now to point to the directory where you'll store the files you build while exploring the system. You can change it later - any time you like. If you do not have a suitable directory, go back to the Windows Program Manager, run the File Manager and create a new one now.

1. From the **File** menu, select **Working Directory**. The **Set Working Directory** dialog box will open, showing the current setting - probably "C:\PDOXWIN\WORKING".

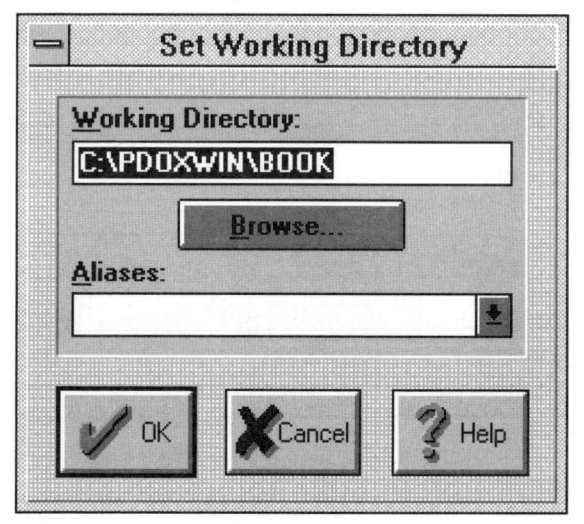

The Browser

Here, as in all situations where you are selecting a file or directory, you can either type in the name, or use the **Browser**. This will display the directory tree.

37

7 Aliases and Directories

2. Double click on the PDOXWIN name to open up its subdirectories (assuming that is where your working directory is), then click the name to select. If you need to switch to a different drive, click on the Down Arrow beside the **Aliases** slot. This holds a list of drives as well as aliases. Select your new drive, then work through the directory tree as before.

3. Exit the Browser with **OK**. This will bring you back to the Set Working Directory window. Click **OK** to save the setting.

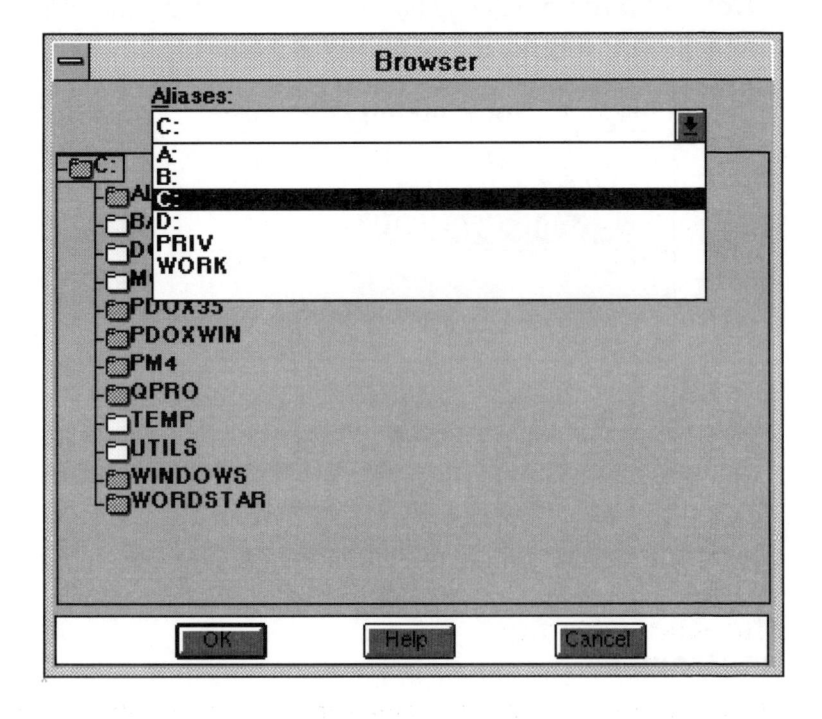

Aliases and Directories 7

Your Private Directory

Some Paradox operations create temporary tables with fixed names. When you run a query to find a group of records, for instance, those records will be stored in a table called ANSWER. We noted earlier that Paradox assumes that you only want this for immediate reference or printing, and at the end of the session it will look for this name and remove the file. This helps to keep the disk free of clutter. If you do want to retain the file for future reference, you can rename it. The important point is, there will only be one ANSWER table at any time - each new query will overwrite it. Now, if you are working on a network, the danger is that someone else's query will overwrite your ANSWER before you have finished with it. Hence the need for a private directory.

Your private directory will store the temporary tables produced by your operations. If you are on a network, set it up now.

1. From the **File** menu select **Private Directory**.

2. Use the Private Directory dialog box as you used that for the Working Directory. The only difference will be at the end of the process. As the private directory is central to many operations, Paradox will have to close down any open files when its setting is changed. You will be asked to confirm that this is OK.

The Alias Manager

There's probably little point in setting up any other new aliases at this stage, but it is worth checking the current definitions.

39

7 Aliases and Directories

1. Select **File** and then **Aliases** to open the **Alias Manager** window. It will almost certainly open with the definition of the alias "PRIV", and its path will be "C:\PDOXWIN\PRIVATE" - unless you have already reset it. The **Driver Type** is "STANDARD", as it always will be unless you are using database drivers other than Paradox or dBase - so most of us can safely ignore this.

2. Click the arrow button beside the **Database Alias** box to pull down the list of current aliases. You should see "PRIV" and "WORK" in there. Click on each of these in turn to check their definitions.

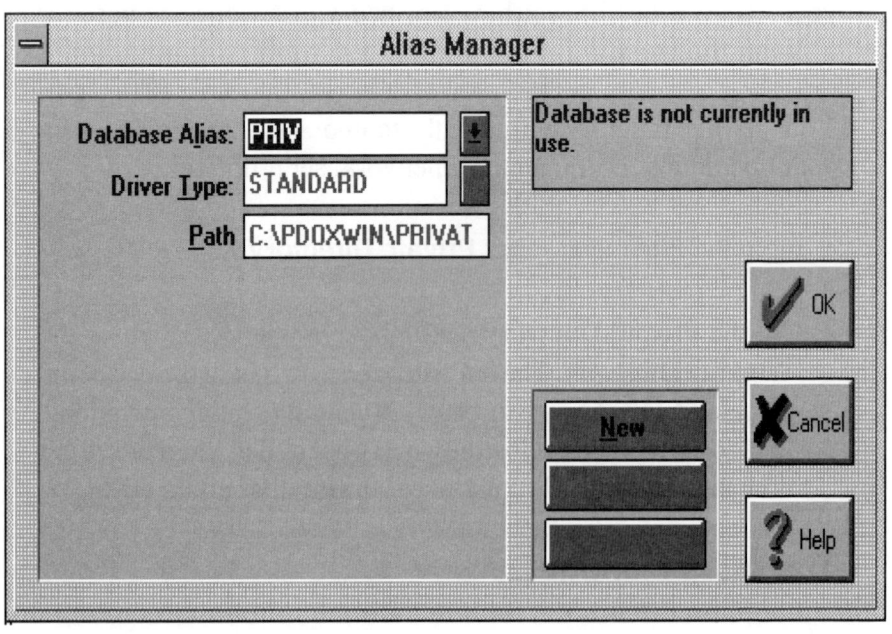

```
                    Alias Manager

    Database Alias: [PRIV      ▼]    Database is not currently in
       Driver Type: [STANDARD    ]   use.
              Path: [C:\PDOXWIN\PRIVAT]

                                           ✓ OK

                        [   New   ]        ✗ Cancel

                        [         ]
                        [         ]        ? Help
```

We'll come back to the Alias Manager later, when we start to work with an example database in a new directory.

40

- 2 -
Working with Single Tables

8 Creating a Database

Database Design

The first stage in setting up any database is to think hard about what information you want to be able to get out of it, and therefore what data you are going to store and in what form. Skimp on this stage and you'll pay for it later!

The Paradox design can be altered easily enough - that's not where the trouble lies. The problem is that when you start to collect data, you might not get all the items that you need, or you get more than is useful, or it has to be reorganised for transfer to the computer. Whatever the case, it wastes time and effort. It will also tend to reduce other people's faith in the system - and therefore their willingness to make full use of it.

Designing the database may be easier in an established business with an existing manual/paper system of data processing. If this is highly organised, it should translate almost directly into computer terms. If, on the other hand, it is a rough and ready system that relies heavily on staff's individual notes and memories, then you might as well start from scratch.

The following sample database is intended to manage the prospective customer files for an estate agency. It is extremely limited as I have only included enough to give a reasonable demonstration - and I'm sure you don't want to do any more typing than is necessary to get the hang of things. If an estate agency does not appeal to you, then adapt it to something more suitable to your own filing needs. Any list of potential or actual clients would have a very similar structure and be used in much the same way.

Creating a Database   8

Information Needs

The database must be able to give us:

- A mailing list of potential buyers when a new house comes on the market.

- An up to date record of where we are in our dealings with the client. Are they still looking? Has an offer been made? Accepted? Contracts exchanged?

- The names of those clients who are still actively looking - if we haven't heard from them in a while, they've probably found something through another agent.

Data Input

By specifying what we want out of the database, we can see what must go in.

- For mailings and other contacts we need the clients' names and addresses. This is obvious, but not to be overlooked. A phone number would also be useful.

- To pick up potential buyers for a house we must know what each client is looking for. We'll record only the maximum price, number of bedrooms and an open ended 'special requirements'. For more realism we might also include type, area, car parking, garden size and other quantifiable factors.

- To track our dealings with the client we will need some kind of status code. This will indicate whether they are looking, making

43

8   Creating a Database

an offer, heading for completion or - finally - satisfied. The name of the agent allocated to the client must also be stored. Later, when we extend the database to include a house file, we will add in a reference for the property being bought, to link the two files.

■ As a check for lost clients, we should record the date of the last contact - and, of course, update this every time we see them.

The Field Structure

We are now in a position to draw up a draft field structure, though to finalise it, we must look at the raw data. Specifically, we know we want to store names and addresses, but how many fields do we need, and of what size?

Names are best split into Surname, Forename or Initials and Title. They can then be sorted into a clear alphabetical order, which will make it easier to find people, and we will have all we need to be able to address their letters properly.

As to the lengths of the fields - err on the side of generosity. Allow for surnames such as "Fotheringay-Smythe" (18 characters), and make the Title field long enough for those couple who prefer to be addressed as "Mr & Mrs" (8 characters).

    Surname :   20 characters   (Alphanumeric data type)
    Initials: 10 characters
    Title :   8 characters

For the address fields, look at your existing files. Take a random selection of a dozen or so and note the lines in each address and the

Creating a Database 8

way that each is organised. They will vary, but is there a pattern that will fit most? Is "Street", "Town" and "County" appropriate? If they vary widely, would you be better with 4 or 5 fields labelled "Address 1", "Address 2", etc? We may later want to be able to search for clients in a particular area or town, so we'll name those fields clearly, but leave others more open ended. We'll make the fields long enough to accommodate any foreseeable combinations.

```
Address 1:    25 characters
Address 2:    25 characters
District :    15 characters
Town:         15 characters
County:       15 characters
```

The other fields are more straightforward.

```
Postcode :    8 characters
Tel. No. :    12 characters
Max Price:    Currency
Bedrooms :    Number
Notes    :    unlimited size - Memo
```

The notes will generally be no more than a few words, and 20 characters or so would probably be enough most of the time. However, there's no point in setting unnecessary restrictions, and a memo field gives us the freedom. Set 20 characters to be stored in the main (.DB) file - and therefore displayed in the table.

```
Last Contact : Date
Status   :    1 character *
```

* The data for the Status field can be in a compact, coded form rather than written out in full. There will be a small space saving, but more

45

8 Creating a Database

importantly, it will reduce typing when data is entered and when making searches. Here we might use the codes:

L	Looking for a property
O	Offer made
A	offer Accepted
C	Contracts exchanged
D	Done!

A set of simple, clear codes - single letters of abbreviations - is a great time saver. They should be easy to remember, but reminders of the codes can be written into the data entry forms, as you will see later.

Defining a New Table 9

Get Paradox up and running. If there are any files left open from earlier explorations, close them down by double clicking their top-left button.

New Table

Click on the leftmost Speed Bar icon, or run through the menu sequence **File|New|Table**. The **Table Type** window will open and offer you **PARADOX** as the type. That is what we want, so click OK.

The **Create Table** window now opens.

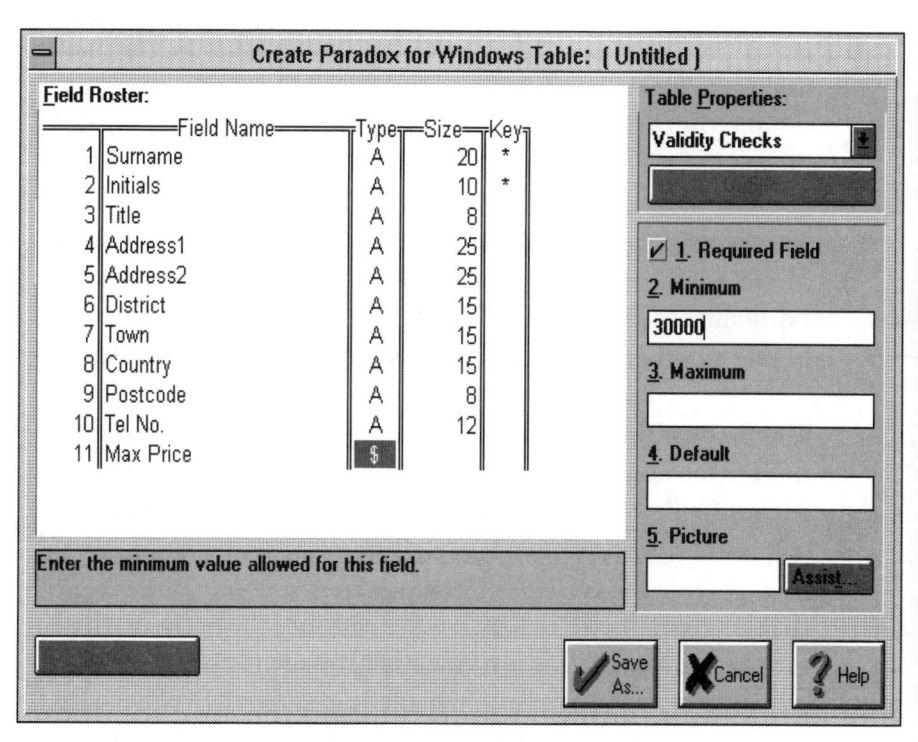

	Field Name	Type	Size	Key
1	Surname	A	20	*
2	Initials	A	10	*
3	Title	A	8	
4	Address1	A	25	
5	Address2	A	25	
6	District	A	15	
7	Town	A	15	
8	Country	A	15	
9	Postcode	A	8	
10	Tel No.	A	12	
11	Max Price	$		

Table Properties: Validity Checks

✓ 1. Required Field
2. Minimum
30000
3. Maximum
4. Default
5. Picture

Enter the minimum value allowed for this field.

Save As... | Cancel | Help

47

9 Defining a New Table

There's quite a lot here, but some of it is irrelevant at this stage, much of it is self-evident and there are helpful prompts to guide you through the process. Don't worry if you make mistakes when you fill in the structure. Fields can be moved, inserted, deleted, renamed or redefined very easily. We'll get back to that later.

The Field Roster

Work through the **Field Roster**, one at a time. When you press **[Enter]** after completing a field, a new line will open up below.

The **Name** can be contain any letters, digits, spaces and symbols apart from the brackets [ ] { } and the combination ->. The main thing is to make the names meaningful, so that they will always remind you of their purpose. Press **[Enter]** after you have written the name, and the highlight bar will move onto the next item.

The **Type** will be one of those discussed in Section 3 - Alphanumeric, Number, ($) Currency, Date, Short Number, Memo, Formatted Memo, Binary, Graphic and OLE. Select it either by typing its initial or pressing **[Spacebar]** and picking from the list.

The **Size** only matters with Alphanumeric fields, where it sets a limit to the number of characters that may be entered, and with Memo fields, where it determines how much of the Memo to display at any one time.

If a field is marked as a **Key** it will determine the order in which records are stored. It is not essential. If there is no key, records will be held in the order in which they are entered. In either case, a file can always be sorted into the order of any field - and re-sorted as often as you like. While you will normally only have one

Defining a New Table 9

Key field in a table, you can have a composite key using several fields. Here, for instance, we are using Surname and Initials. Set both of these as Keys and it will put the file in telephone directory order.

Key fields must be at the top of the roster, and with composite keys, the most important one goes first. To set (or remove) a key, press [Spacebar] or double-click with the cursor in the Key column.

Validity Checks

Up in the top right you will see the heading **Table Properties**, and beneath this a highlighted **Validity Checks**. The various checks are then listed in the panel beneath. These allow you to control the nature of the data that is entered into any chosen fields. There are several options, and they can be set singly or in combination.

To place a check on a field, click anywhere on its line in the roster to select the field. Now turn to the main panel on the right.

> **Required Field** - if set, data must be entered into the field before the record will be accepted. In the example, the Required Fields must include Surname, Initials, Address 1, Town, Postcode, Max Price, Last Contact and Status. If you feel that any others are also essential, then make them Required. Don't overdo it! Sometimes the data may not be available and then you would be unable to enter the record. To set this check, click on the button beside the name to make a tick appear.
>
> **Minimum** and **Maximum** set limits on the values in number fields. It would be useful to set a Minimum here to pick up

49

9   Defining a New Table

unrealistic values caused by typing errors. Click on the Max Price line, then move to the **Minimum** slot and type in a suitable value. Hereabouts you'll get nothing under £30,000 - and precious little for that!

Default values will be placed into a field if no other data is entered there. We could usefully set a Default for the Status field, as almost every new client will start at the same place. Select Status and set "L" (for Looking) as the Default. That will save us from having to type it in for each new record.

The **Picture** check is used to format data. It defines the kind of characters that can be entered and can force them to upper case. There are several control characters, of which the most useful are **#**, which insists on a digit, **&**, which converts to upper case and **?**, which accepts any letter. For example:

Picture	Data Format	
###.##	123.45	
&&&	ABC	(entered as "abc", "Abc" or "ABC")
&?????	Smith	(first letter only capitalised)

This is the most complex of the validity checks, which is no doubt why there is an **Assist** menu with some sample pictures. Used properly, it can make data entry fairly foolproof, but is perhaps best left until you're more at ease with the system.

Validity Checks are only one item in the Table Properties menu. Others cover passwords, indexing and cross-referencing. Explore them if you have time, otherwise let's wrap this up and start to get some data in.

Defining a New Table 9

Check Your Definition

Go over the fields one last time. Highlight each in turn and make sure that if a validity check is set for the field, you have the correct information in the right panel. Retype any field names or definitions if you find a mistype, and reset the checks if necessary. When you are satisfied that all is well, save the table. (See next section.) With the file safe on disk, you could then close down if you want to take a break.

10   Saving and Opening Files

All major objects - Tables, Forms, Queries, Reports, Scripts and Mail Merge documents - can be stored on disk as files, and are saved and opened in much the same way. The relevant commands are all on the **File** menu, and - as we have already seen - when you create a new object, the Save option is offered automatically.

Save

With Paradox, you will normally only save a table when you first define it, or after you have restructured it or changed its properties. You never need to save it after data entry, for the data is saved automatically each time a record is entered or changed.

When you are saving a file for the first time, this will open the **Save Table As..** dialog box. There you will select the directory in which to store the file, and give a name to identify it. With an existing file, **Save** simply replaces the old disk file with the updated version, without any further work on your part.

Filenames

The rules for filenames are the same as in all Windows/MS-DOS applications. It must have no more than 8 characters and may not include spaces or any punctuation symbols apart from the underline. **Do Not give extensions.** Paradox will automatically add extensions to identify the nature of the files - **.DB** for database tables, **.RSL** for Report definitions, and so on.

On a purely practical level, it helps if you keep all names clear, meaningful and with simple spelling.

Saving and Opening Files   10

Save your table definition now.

1. Click on the **Save As** button. This opens the **Save Table As** dialog box. Check that the **Path** is pointing to the right directory - it will generally be WORK, your current working directory.

2. Type in a suitable name, such as "CLIENTS" - but don't press [Enter] yet!

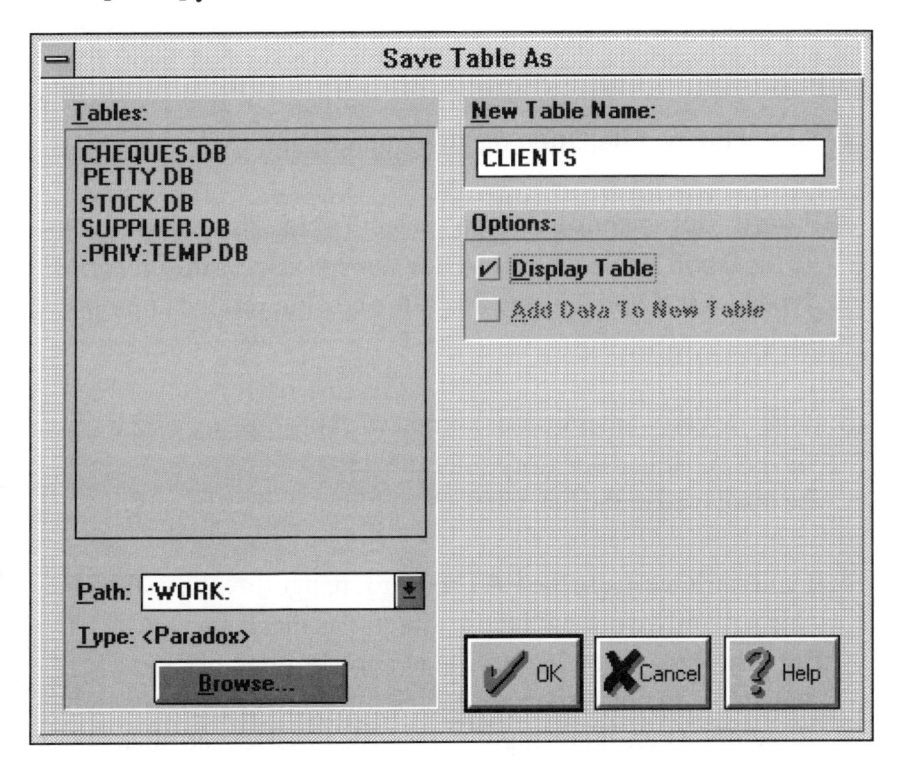

```
                        Save Table As
Tables:                         New Table Name:
 CHEQUES.DB                      CLIENTS
 PETTY.DB
 STOCK.DB                       Options:
 SUPPLIER.DB
 :PRIV:TEMP.DB                    ✓ Display Table
                                  ☐ Add Data To New Table




Path: :WORK:
Type: <Paradox>
       Browse...              ✓ OK   ✗ Cancel   ? Help
```

3. In the **Options** panel on the right you will see a little button marked **Display Table**. Click on this if you want to go straight to data entry after saving the table. Finally, click OK.

53

10 Saving and Opening Files

The file will be saved as "CLIENTS.DB". Paradox adds the "DB" extension, to indicate that this is a database table. As you will see later, other objects have different extensions to identify their natures.

Open

Use this to bring a file back onto the Desktop. If you didn't set the Display Table option, or if you have closed and restarted since the last section, work through these steps now to open the Clients file.

1. Start with the **File|Open** menu sequence.

2. From the sub-menu of file types, select **Table**. This will take you to the **Open Table** dialog box. (When you select a different file type to open, you will see this same box but retitled appropriately.)

3. If the file you want is in your normal working directory - and you haven't changed directory since the start of your session - it will be displayed in the list. Click to highlight it, then press OK.

4. If you can't see it, use the **PATH** slot to change directory - though this will only work with those directories that have an Alias. If for any reason, you have a file in another directory - and it is unlikely - do not despair. Use the Browser to move to the right directory. Once there, highlight the file to select and click OK.

5. The table will brought onto the Desktop, ready for viewing or editing.

Saving and Opening Files 10

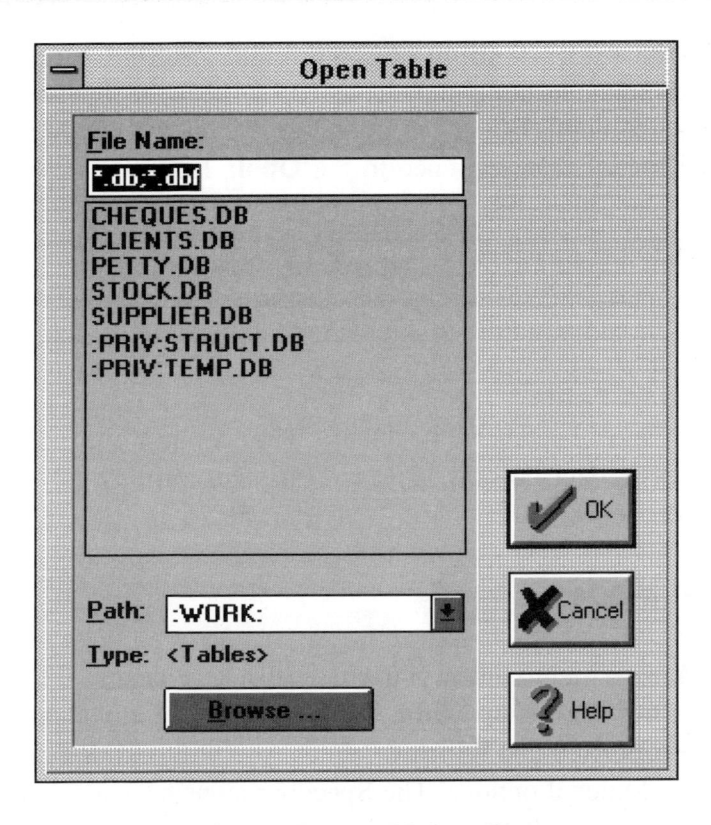

The Open Table Dialog Box

11 Adding and Editing Records

If you have just come from the Create routine, with the Display Table option set, you should now have the CLIENTS table open on the Desktop. If not, click on the **Open Table** icon, or work through the **File|Open|Table** sequence to the **Open Table** dialog box and select the Clients file.

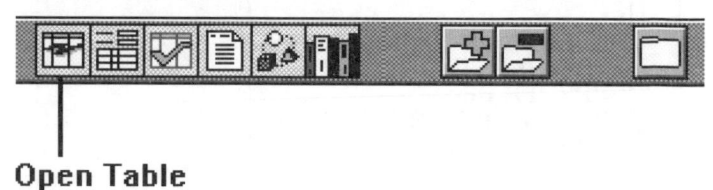

Open Table

However you get there, the table will be open in **View** mode - you can see the data, but not change it. To do that, you must get into **Edit** mode.

Edit Mode

Look at the Menu bar and you will see that it has changed. There are now three new menus - **Edit, Table** and **Record**. If you pull down the **Properties** and **Window** menus, you will find that they now have additional options. The Speedbar icons have also changed. There are a whole lot of new functions up there, that are available when a table is open and active. We'll work through most of them over the next few sections. For the moment, just notice those labelled on the figure.

The **Cut, Copy** and **Paste** icons access the normal Windows Cut-and-Paste facilities, and work in the usual way. Highlight a field, or set of fields and the data in them can be cut or copied to the Clipboard - either for transfer to another application or to elsewhere within Paradox.

Adding and Editing Records 11

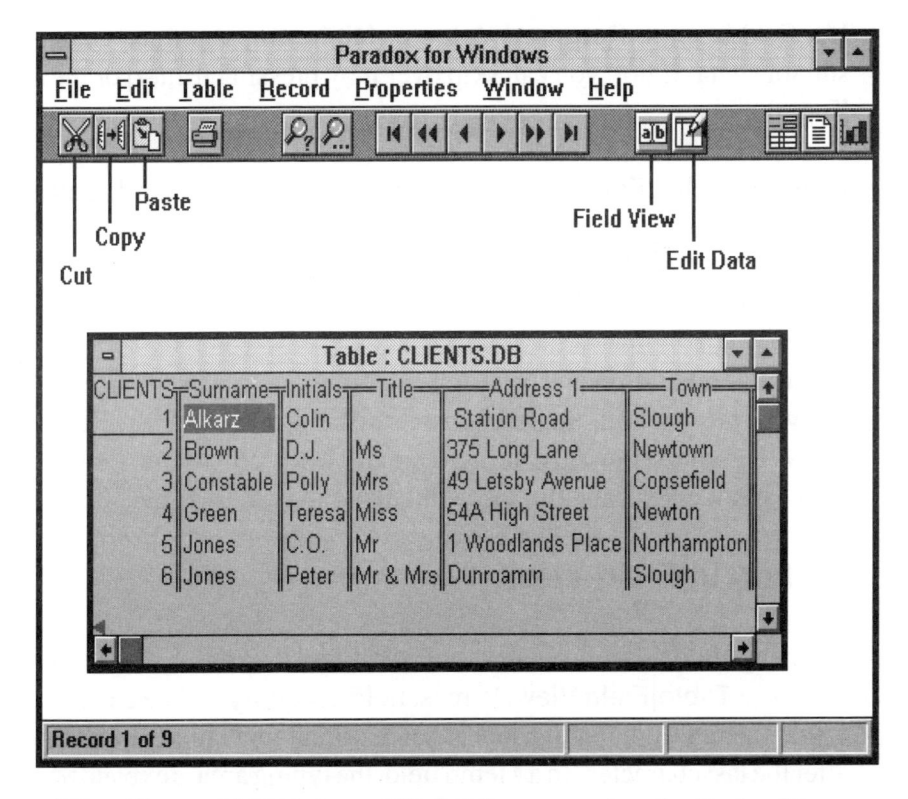

![Screenshot of Paradox for Windows showing the CLIENTS.DB table with toolbar labels: Cut, Copy, Paste, Field View, Edit Data]

We will want **Edit Data** and **Field View** very shortly. Both of these can also be access from the **Table** menu, and they have Function key alternatives, if you prefer.

Get the table into Edit mode now with **Edit Data.**

Editing Data

On a new table, the first field of the first record will be highlighted, waiting for you to enter data. Type in the surname, rubbing out errors with [Backspace], if necessary, then press [Enter]. The highlight will move onto the next field.

57

11 Adding and Editing Records

If a field is set to **Required Value** or **Minimum**, you must enter suitable data. If not, you can skip over it by pressing [Enter] or the [Right] arrow.

In the last field, [Enter] will take you down to the next record. You can also move to the next record from any other field, by pressing the [Down] arrow - though Paradox will not let you go if you have left a Required field blank.

To edit a field, after data has been entered there, use the mouse or arrow keys to move the highlight bar to the field, then switch to **Field View**. This mode must also be used for any work with Memo fields. You cannot enter data into these or edit data them in Table View.

Editing in Field View

To change into this mode, click the **Field View** icon or use the menu sequence **Table|Field View**. In most fields, the only visible change is that the highlight bar disappears and a small text cursor appears after the last character. In a Memo field, the typing area is expanded into a whole window.

If you want to **change the whole entry**, then simply type it in. The existing entry will disappear with the first character that you type.

For **minor edits**, move the cursor to the right place, remove unwanted characters and type in new data.

In this mode, the keys move the cursor within the field, rather than between fields.

Adding and Entering Records 11

Keys in Field View

[Left]	move one character left;
[Right]	move one character right;
[Home]	move to start of field;
[End]	move to end of field;
[Delete]	delete character to the right of the cursor;
[Backspace]	delete left, as in Edit mode;
[Enter]	ends the edit.

There are a couple of variations that apply only to Memo fields:

[Up]	move up one line;
[Down]	move down one line;
[Enter]	start a new line within the Memo.

From a Memo field, exit from Field View the same way you came in - click the icon or use the Table menu. From other fields, press [Enter] or use the mouse to move the cursor to another field.

Moving Between Records

There are several alternatives open here. With a small table, it is probably simplest to scroll the table with the window sliders, but that gets a bit hit-and-miss beyond a certain limit. For more controlled movement, use the **Record** menu, or the set of icons on the left of the Speedbar. They have an identical range of functions and their meanings are largely obvious.

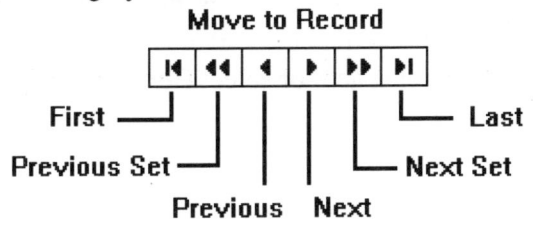

```
              Move to Record
         |◄|◄◄| ◄ | ▶ |▶▶|▶|
   First ─┘   │   │   │   └─ Last
Previous Set ─┘   │   └─ Next Set
              Previous  Next
```

59

11 Adding and Editing Records

The arrow icons on the Speedbar probably offer the simplest way to browse through a file. Hold down on the **Next** or **Previous** arrows to run smoothly - and rapidly - through the file one record at a time. Click them for a single move. In **Previous Set** and **Next Set**, the *Set* is a windowful. If 10 rows are displayed at a time, then these will take you backwards or forwards 10 records. We'll look at the Locate functions - the Magnifying Glass icons - separately later in Section 16.

If you are editing, you may find it more convenient to move between records using the keyboard.

[Arrows]	Up or Down to adjacent records;
	Left or Right to adjacent fields;
[Home]	first field of current record;
[End]	last field of current record;
[Pg Up]	back one screenful;
[Pg Dn]	forward one screenful;
[Ctrl] [Home]	first field of first record;
[Ctrl] [End]	last field of last record;
[Ctrl] [Pg Up]	left one screen width;
[Ctrl] [Pg Dn]	right one screen width.

Deleting a Record

If you want to delete a record, or abandon an entry because you have written in so many mistakes that it is not worth the effort of correcting them, make sure that the cursor is on the right line, then either press [Ctrl] [Backspace] or select **Record|Delete**.

Adding and Editing Records   11

Sample Data

You will need some sample data for some of the things that we'll be trying out later. Half a dozen or so records will be enough, and the less important fields can be left blank. You want a range of values, with some items the same. This is the sample data I shall be using. You may like to copy it in, or create your own data along similar lines.

Mr Colin Alkarz   Station Road   Slough
Max Price: £150,000 Beds : 6 Last Contact : 30/04/92   Status : L
Ms D.J. Brown   375 Long Lane   Newtown
Max Price: £175,000 Beds : 6 Last Contact : 12/04/92   Status : O
Mrs Polly Constable 49 Letsby Avenue   Copsefield
Max Price: £100,000 Beds : 4 Last Contact : 15/05/92   Status : O
Miss Teresa Green 54A High Street Newton
Max Price: £45,000 Beds : 2 Last Contact : 17/05/92   Status : L
Mr C.O. Jones   1 Woodlands Place   Northampton
Max Price: £75,000 Beds : 5 Last Contact : 19/05/92   Status : L
Mr & Mrs Peter Jones   Dunroamin   Slough
Max Price: £75,000 Beds : 3 Last Contact : 16/05/92   Status : A
Mr Bill Sergeant   23 Station Road   Newton
Max Price: £80,000 Beds : 4 Last Contact : 21/05/92   Status : L
Mr & Mrs W.H. Smith   17 Church Lane   Old Newton
Max Price: £75,000 Beds : 2 Last Contact : 12/05/92   Status : L
Mr A.B. Smyth   12 The Avenue   Romsey
Max Price: £125,000 Beds : 4 Last Contact : 21/05/92   Status : L

11 Adding and Editing Records

Leaving Edit Mode

When you have done, you can return to View mode by clicking on the Edit Mode icon, or take the menu sequence **Table|End Edit**. If you prefer, you can simply clear the table off the Desktop by clicking on the top left button and selecting **Close** from the Control Menu.

There is no need to save the table. This is done automatically when you exit from Edit mode.

Altering the Table Layout 12

The order that fields appear in the roster may not be the best order in which to enter or view the data on screen. You may also find that some fields are inconveniently wide.

Moving Fields

Fields can be easily moved to different columns. It won't change the roster order, nor affect any data that may be there - it simply alters the image. To move a field:

1. Take the cursor to the title line at the top of the table. The cursor will change to a small box when it is in the right position.

2. Hold down the left button, and the cursor will change again - this time to a double-headed black arrow.

3. Drag the arrow left or right to where you want the field, then release it.

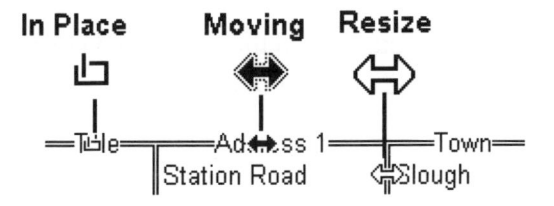

```
   In Place      Moving     Resize
      ┌┐           ⬥          ⟺
       │           │           │
   ═Table═══   ═Address 1═  ═Town═
            ║Station Road    ⟸Slough
```

Changing Field Widths

With fields such as addresses, you need to allow a large number of characters so that they can cope with lengthy street and town names. In practice, most addresses are take only part of the available space, but those wide columns mean that few fields are visible at any one

63

12 Altering the Table Layout

time. By shrinking the widths, you may trim the display of a few items, but at least be able to see all the whole address for most people. There's no data loss - all the characters are stored in the database, even if only 10 are visible at a time on screen.

If the field has a long name, its column will be as wide as is necessary to accommodate the title. This may be significantly wider than the data to be stored in it. The **Status** field, in the example, has a 6 character name, but stores only a single character. If you want to squeeze more fields into view, and don't mind sacrificing the title display, then shrink those fields. To adjust the width of a field:

1. First find a group of records where the lengths of the data items are reasonably representative, so that you know how far you can shrink the field without losing too much data.

2. Move the cursor to the top of the right hand boundary of the field. The cursor will change to a double-headed white arrow when it is in the right position.

3. Hold down the left button and the right-hand boundary will be highlighted. It's ready to be moved.

4. Drag the arrow left to shrink the field or right to widen it. A shadow of the boundary line will move with the cursor. Compare this against the data items to ensure that you set a suitable width.

Using Forms   13

Tables give a compact presentation and are the best way to hunt through the file when you are looking for items in a particular field. However, it is not a convenient way to look at any one record - unless it has so few fields that it will fit within the width of the window. For a better view of individual records, you need a Form.

Quick Form

This function will generate a simple form for use with the current table - you must have a table open for viewing or editing at the time. Click the icon in the Speedbar, or select **Table|Quick Form** from the menus.

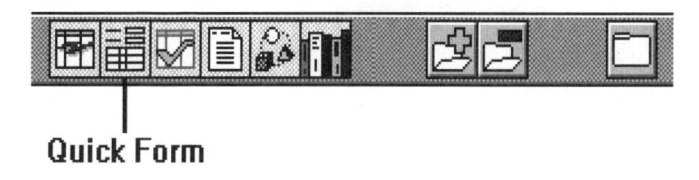

Quick Form

The form will be a straight vertical listing of the fields, possibly in two columns, with each field labelled with its name. It's all ready to use, but it could do with improvement. The order that arises from the layout is not necessarily the most convenient order in which to enter data; there's nothing to make the more important fields stand out; and your users may well need some explanatory text. None of these present major problems.

Once you have found your way around the design menus and tools, it only takes a few minutes to pull a form into a more attractive and usable shape. We'll return to that in the next section. For the moment, let's stick with the Quick Form - it's sometimes good enough for the job, and the techniques for using forms are the same whatever their design.

13 Using Forms

When the form first opens it will be in View mode - you can see the data, but not change it. Note the new icons on the Speedbar. **Table View** will take you back to your table; **Design** will take you to Design mode - of which more shortly.

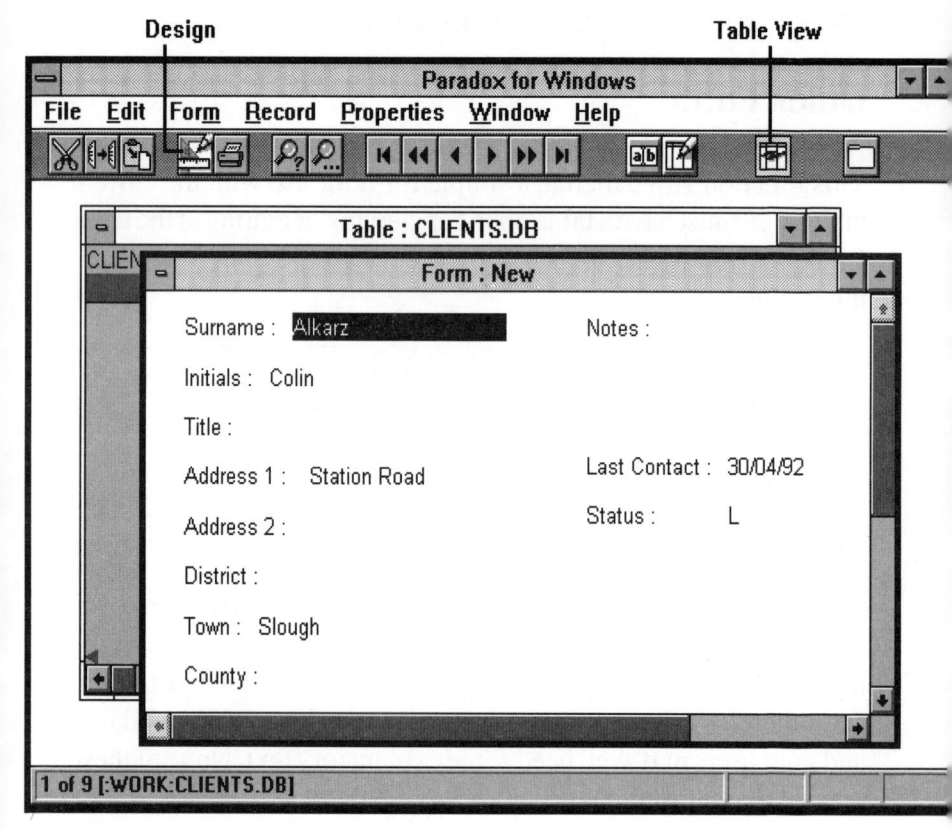

Movement in Forms

If you are using the mouse, movement here is the same as in Table View. If the form is larger than its window - as is often the case - use the scroll bars to bring different parts into view. Pull a new record onto the form using the Speedbar arrows or the Record menu.

Using Forms 13

The keyboard controls are somewhat different from those in Table View..

[Arrows]	move between fields on the current form;
[Enter]	move to next field; *
[Home]	first field;
[End]	last field;
[Pg Up]	previous record;
[Pg Dn]	next record;
[Ctrl] [Home]	first field of first record;
[Ctrl] [End]	last field of last record;
[Ctrl] [Pg Up]	left one screen width;
[Ctrl] [Pg Dn]	right one screen width.

* Note: the "next" field isn't necessarily the next one in the field roster. Movement follows the logic of the design - left to right and down the form.

Data Entry and Editing on Forms

Switch to Edit mode by clicking the Edit Data icon, or with the menu sequence **Form|Edit Data**. Editing is exactly the same as in a table. Use Field View for editing within a field and for any memo fields.

When you are finished, return to View mode by clicking the Lightning icon, or with the menu sequence **Form|End Edit**.

67

14   Designing a Form

There are two different methods of creating a form. You've already met one - clicking on **Quick Form** when you are working with a table. This is the simplest, and the best for a general purpose form. The other way is through the menu sequence **File|New|Form**. Here you have to do everything for yourself, but there's a lot more flexibility on overall layout and style. We'll leave this until we need more specialised forms.

With the initial Quick Form in view, click on the **Design** icon on the right of the Speedbar, or select **Form|Design** from the menus. In the Design mode, a new set of tools appears on the Speedbar and the Form window has rulers to help with accurate size and placings.

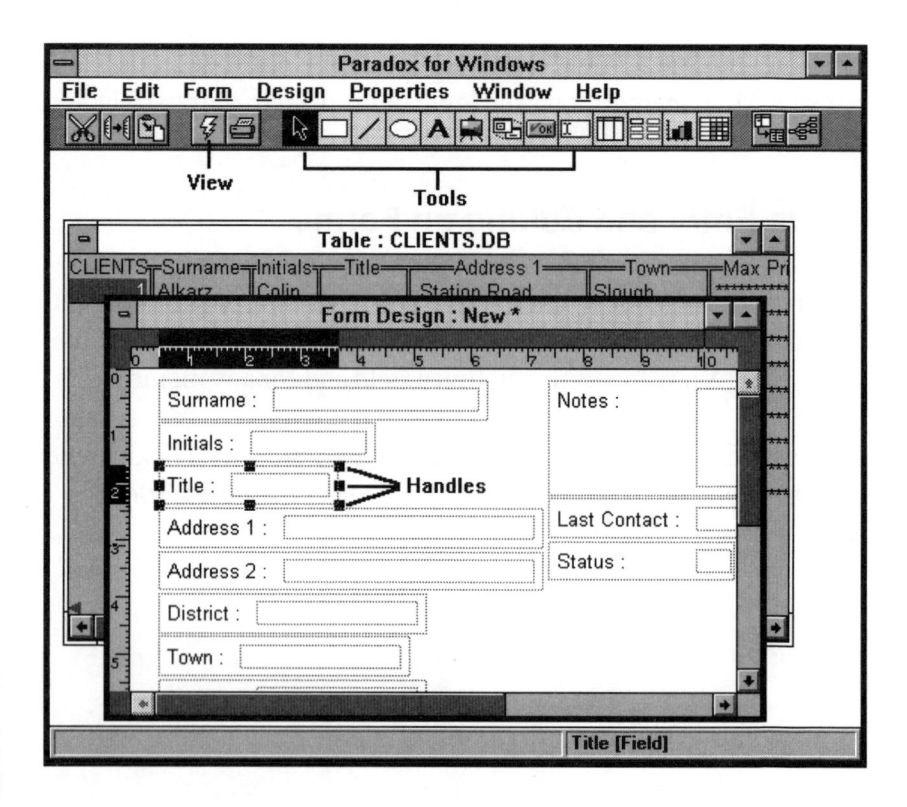

Designing a Form 14

On the form, each field is represented by a dotted outline, enclosed along with its label in a larger outline. The field itself, its label and the enclosing outline can all be moved and their sizes changed independently - though with the restriction that the label and field must remain within the outline, and if you move the outline, its contents go with it.. As with every Paradox object, all three have properties which can be accessed from their menu. (See next Section). But before you can move, resize or change the properties, you must first select the object.

- To **select the outer rectangle**, click once anywhere inside the area. The **handles** will then appear, and outline can be moved or altered.

- To **select the label or the data area**, point to it and double-click - a single click will do if the outer rectangle is already highlighted.

Once an object has been selected:

- **Move** it by pointing the cursor inside the outline and dragging.

- **Change its size** by dragging on a handle.

- Pull down its **Properties menu** by right clicking on the object.

A group of objects can be selected together, so that they can then all be moved or their properties changed together.

To **select a group of objects**:

1. Left-click on the first - to get the handles;

2. Hold down **[Shift]** and click on all the other objects you want to select - handles will appear on each.

14 Designing a Form

The Design Tools

There is a full set of **Tools** for enhancing the appearance of the form, though you would be advised to stick to the text and drawing tools at first.

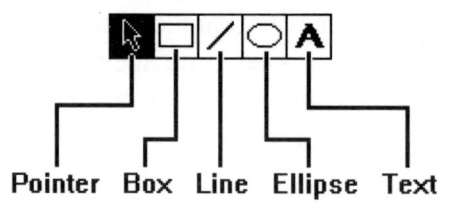

```
Pointer  Box  Line  Ellipse  Text
```

Box, Line & Ellipse

A **Box** dropped around a field, or set of related fields, will help to focus attention on them, and therefore make it easier to locate items on screen. To create a box:

1. Click the box icon in the Speedbar;

2. Move to the top left corner of where you want it and click;

3. Drag the outline to pull the box into shape.

4. Exit from box-drawing by clicking on the Pointer (or any other) tool.

The box can then be moved or reshaped in exactly the same way as a field outline. When you move it, all the objects inside the box are normally moved as well, which can make restructuring much easier.

Lines and **Ellipses** are created and handled in much the same way as Boxes. When you adjust a line, you can move it by dragging from anywhere along its length, or change its length or angle by dragging one of the handles.

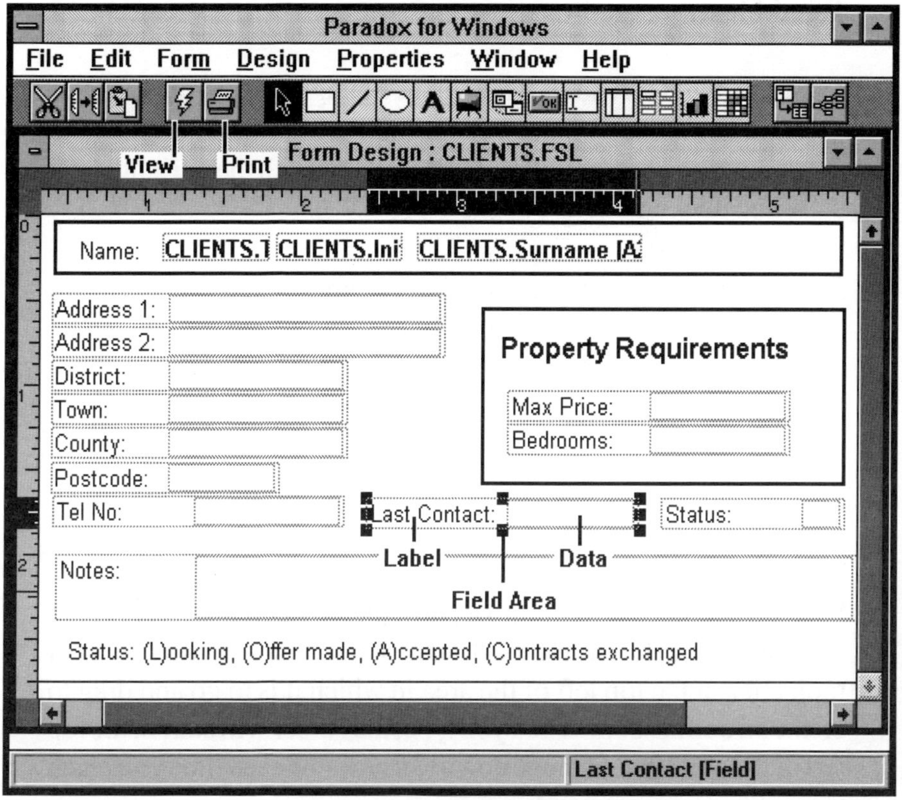
Paradox for Windows
File Edit Form Design Properties Window Help
View
Print
Form Design : CLIENTS.FSL
Name:
CLIENTS.T
CLIENTS.Ini
CLIENTS.Surname [A
Address 1:
Address 2:
District:
Town:
County:
Postcode:
Tel No:
Property Requirements
Max Price:
Bedrooms:
Last Contact:
Status:
Notes:
Label
Data
Field Area
Status: (L)ooking, (O)ffer made, (A)ccepted, (C)ontracts exchanged
Last Contact [Field]

Text

Headings, notes and "small print" can all be added freely to a form, using the Text tool. There are several examples of this on the form shown on the next page. You will see that a heading has been added to the "Property Requirements" group of fields; that the Surname, Initials and Title fields have all had their individual labels removed and a new "Name" heading substituted; and that coding notes for the Status field have been written at the bottom.

14 Designing a Form

To add text:

1. Select the **Text** tool. The cursor changes to the add-a-letter combination **+A**. Point to where you want the text and click. The new writing cursor will be located in line with the upright of the + and above bottom of the A.

2. Type, using [Backspace] to correct errors, and [Enter] to move the cursor down for a second line.

3. When you have finished, click anywhere else on the screen.

4. If the text object is not in the right place, highlight it and drag it to its new position.

If you want the text to fit into a particular area on the screen, then use a slightly different approach at the start. After selecting the Text tool, click at the top left of the area in which it is to go and drag to create an outline box. When you type, the cursor will start in the top left of the outline, and move down to a new line each time you reach the right edge.

When you are reasonably satisfied with the design, switch to Edit mode either by clicking the Lightning icon, or with the menu sequence **Form|Edit Data**. The appearance of the working form may not be quite what you wanted - there are some subtle differences between the Design and Edit modes. It's not a problem. You can go back into Design mode and adjust it as often and whenever you like. In Paradox, every object has a set of Properties, that determine its appearance - colour, font, size, line thickness or whatever. Don't ignore these when designing forms, for they can make a form more

Designing a Form   14

effective as well as more attractive. A different colour for text or background, a heavier font, varying thicknesses of line can all help to focus attention on key parts of the form. But don't overdo it. The secret of good design is restraint. Pick out one item with colour or a bolder, larger font and the reader's eye will be drawn to it. Make every item startlingly different, and your users won't know where to look - and may prefer to look elsewhere!

There is also a good practical reason for keeping your designs simple. The more you add by way of fancy fonts, extra text, boxes, lines and - especially - graphics, the more you slow the system down.

The finished form should look something like this - or better!

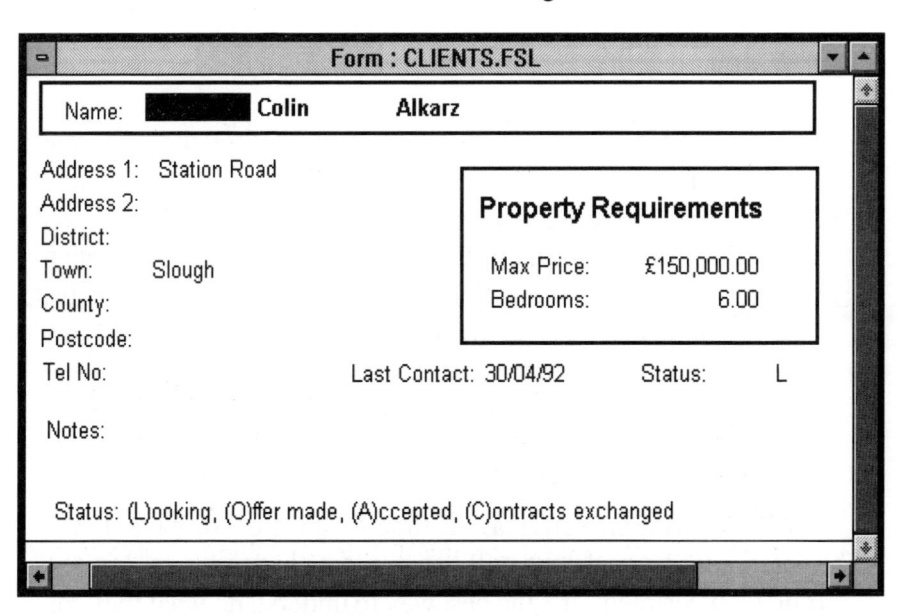

```
┌─────────────────────────────────────────────────────────┐
│ ▢              Form : CLIENTS.FSL                    ▼▲ │
│  ┌───────────────────────────────────────────────────┐  │
│  │ Name:    ▓▓▓▓▓▓▓ Colin     Alkarz                 │  │
│  └───────────────────────────────────────────────────┘  │
│ Address 1:  Station Road                                │
│ Address 2:              ┌─────────────────────────────┐ │
│ District:               │ Property Requirements       │ │
│ Town:       Slough      │                             │ │
│ County:                 │ Max Price:     £150,000.00  │ │
│ Postcode:               │ Bedrooms:             6.00  │ │
│ Tel No:                 └─────────────────────────────┘ │
│                    Last Contact: 30/04/92   Status:   L │
│ Notes:                                                  │
│                                                         │
│ Status: (L)ooking, (O)ffer made, (A)ccepted, (C)ontracts exchanged │
│                                                       ▼ │
│ ◀                                                    ▶  │
└─────────────────────────────────────────────────────────┘
```

73

15 Properties and Design

Each object on the form has its own **Properties** menu. The form itself, every field, label and data entry region, box, line, ellipse and block of text - all can be individually adjusted. You can also change the properties for a group of objects in one go - very useful if you want to change the font on a whole set of fields.

How you get the menu depends upon the object.

- With the background, boxes, field outlines and other free-standing objects, point within their area and right-click.

- With objects inside boxes or other outlines, first double-click to highlight them, then right-click for the menu.

- With a group of objects, right-click on any of the selected ones.

Properties vary according to the nature of the object, though some are common to many and the menu operations are always the same. Some propertiy options are **toggles** - on/off switches. If they are on, there will be a tick beside them. Click on the option's name to change from on to off or vice versa. Some options have their own menus. These are indicated by an arrowhead on the right hand side. Click on the name to open the sub-menu. Paradox assumes you only want to change one property at a time and closes down the menu(s) once you have made a selection.

You can redefine properties at any time - even after you have started to enter records - and none will put your data in danger, so don't be afraid to experiment. It's the best way to understand what they can do.

Properties and Design   15

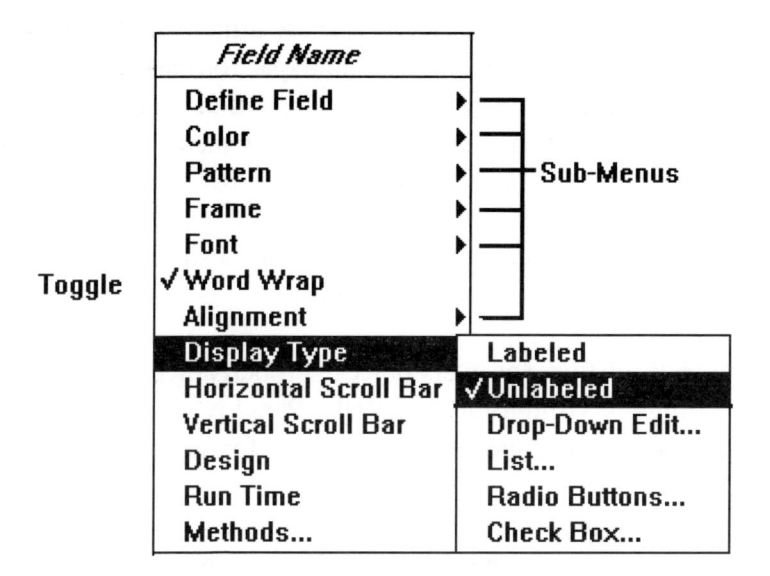

```
              Field Name
              Define Field      ▶
              Color             ▶
              Pattern           ▶ ── Sub-Menus
              Frame             ▶
              Font              ▶
  Toggle   √ Word Wrap
              Alignment         ▶
              Display Type         Labeled
              Horizontal Scroll Bar  √ Unlabeled
              Vertical Scroll Bar    Drop-Down Edit...
              Design               List...
              Run Time             Radio Buttons...
              Methods...           Check Box...
```

Field Properties

Right-click on a field and have a look what's on the menu. Here are a few of the more significant properties.

■ **Frame, Color,** and **Pattern** are all display enhancers. Use one or more of these to highlight a field.

■ **Word Wrap** determines what happens to text that is too long to fit across the width of its allocated space. If it is toggled ON, extra words are taken down to a lower line - if one is available.

■ **Display Type** has a number of options. The key ones are probably the first two - do you want the field to be Labelled or Unlabelled. Normally you would want the label, but sometimes you will want to remove it and add clearer text instead.

15 Properties and Design

■ **Horizontal** and **Vertical Scroll Bar** are principally for memo and graphic fields, where the available space on the form may be smaller than the object in the field. These options add scroll bars, to give the user a simple way of examining the object.

■ **Design** lets you fasten the field to the form to prevent it from being moved accidentally. You can pin its position in either or both the horizontal and vertical planes.

■ **Methods** are found on every object's property menu. A method is a program written in ObjectPal - Paradox's programming language. We will leave these well alone for the time being.

■ The **Run Time** sub-menu controls the display during use. You can generally ignore these, but there are a couple of options that you might find of interest:

■ **Run Time|Tab Stop** When turned on, you can move onto this field using the Tab key. Turn it off to make the Tab jump over the field.

■ **Run Time|No echo** is for passwords and ultra-sensitive data. If this is turned on, the data is not displayed on screen when it is typed, or ever after.

■ **Format** appears on the menu for Number fields. The sub-menu from this holds a set of 8 built-in formats for numbers. There should normally be one here that will produce an acceptable result. If you do have special needs, click on the [..] bar at the top. This will take you to a dialog box where you can define the format in terms on number of decimal places, punctuation, how to display negative values and the like.

Properties and Design 15

Number Formats

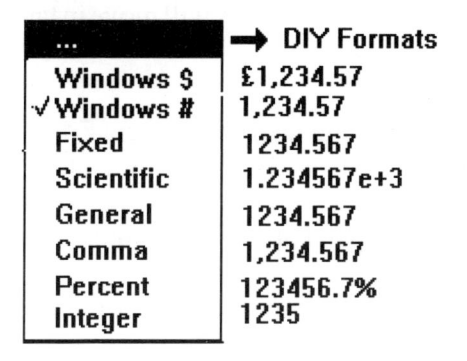

...	→ DIY Formats
Windows $	£1,234.57
√ Windows #	1,234.57
Fixed	1234.567
Scientific	1.234567e+3
General	1234.567
Comma	1,234.567
Percent	123456.7%
Integer	1235

With **Fixed**, you set the number of decimal places that you want.

Scientific is for very large - or very small - numbers. To convert them back to 'real' numbers, move the decimal point according to the exponent value (e). e+3 means times 10^3, or three places to the right; e-7 would mean divide by 10^7, or move the point 7 places left - filling out with 0s as necessary.

General shows values as they are typed in, or in Scientific format if the number is too large to fit in the available space.

Comma places a comma between the thousands.

Percent multiplies the number by 100 and adds the % sign. Use it only for fractions.

Integer rounds any fractions to the nearest whole number.

Try the Properties menus for different fields. You might also like to explore the properties of other objects.

15 Properties and Design

On the **Box** menu, watch out for **Contain Objects**. Toggle this on and the fields and text within the box will move in tandem when you drag the box to a new site.

On the **Text Properties** menu, try a different **Font**. The sub-menu lets you change its Typeface, Size, Style or Colour.

The **Typeface** will depend upon your printer.

Size will typically vary from 2 to 72 - again, depending upon your system.

The **Style** can be **Bold**, *Italic*, Strikeout (never seen the point of that myself) or Underline.

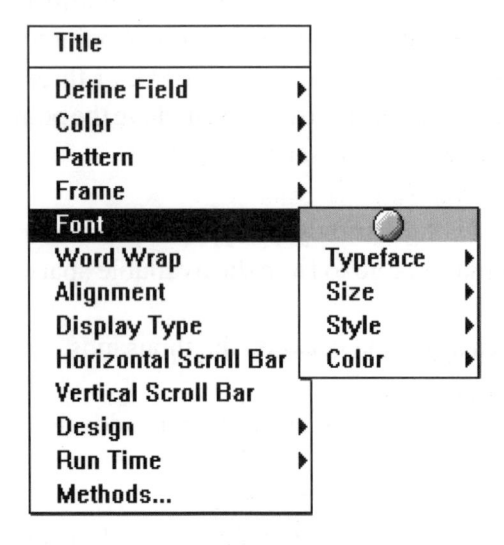

```
Title
Define Field        ▶
Color               ▶
Pattern             ▶
Frame               ▶
Font                      ○
Word Wrap              Typeface   ▶
Alignment              Size       ▶
Display Type           Style      ▶
Horizontal Scroll Bar  Color      ▶
Vertical Scroll Bar
Design              ▶
Run Time            ▶
Methods...
```

When you think you have finished, return to edit mode and have a good look at the form. If you have overdone the enhancements - an easy trap to fall into - go back into design mode and tone them down.

78

Searching 16

With fewer than a dozen items in our sample database, we can find anything we want by simply browsing through it. With a real database, browsing is rarely a viable option. You need a more directed method of searching for data. There are essentially two approaches to this.

If you want to look up records to view or edit their data, you would do it via a **Locate**.

Where you want to pull out a set of records for closer scrutiny, or to print as a report, you would do it via a **Query**.

Let's start with the simpler **Locate**.

Locating Values

This is the main searching facility. It will hunt through the database, looking for a defined value in one field - for instance, finding the records where the Name is 'Jones'.

You can run the search from either Form or Table view.

1. Use the menu sequence **Record|Locate Value**, or click on the left-hand magnifying glass icon.

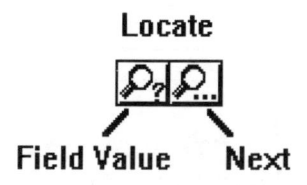

   Locate

   Field Value   Next

2. The process starts in the **Locate Value** dialog box. Set the cursor in the **Value** box and type in the target data, then click the

79

16 Searching

Fields button to get the list of fields. Selection from this list is a bit tricky. Only a few fields are displayed at a time.

3. If the one you want is not visible, drag the highlight bar to the bottom (or top) of the list and try to take it further. The field list will then scroll beneath the cursor.

4. Highlight the field in which the required value will be found.

5. Type in the value to be searched for, setting the **Case** and **Match** options as necessary.

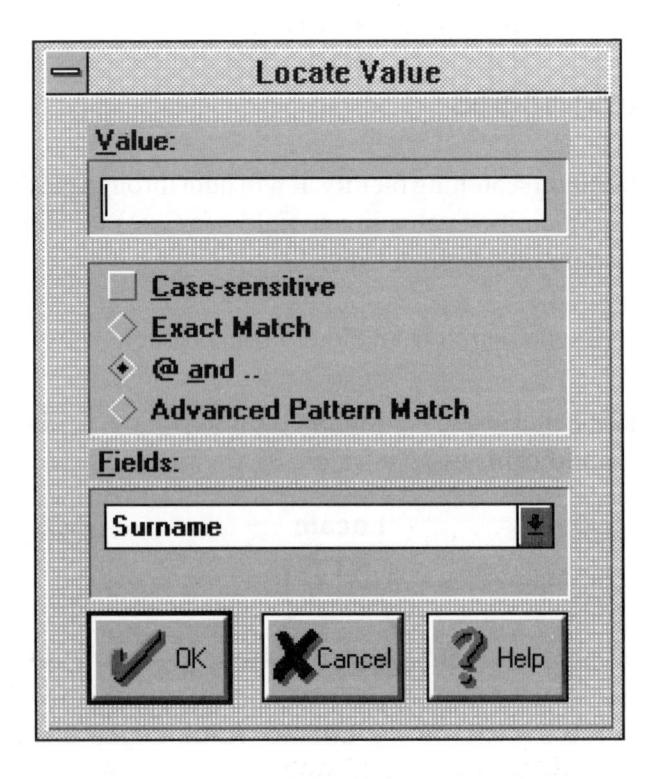

Searching 16

When the **Case Sensitive** option is left unset, Paradox makes no distinction between lower and upper case letters. e.g. 'smith' would find 'smith','Smith' and 'SMITH'. Only set this on those rare occasions where case is crucial.

The **Exact Match** and **@ and ..** options are two sides of the same coin, both relating to the use of **wildcards**. A wildcard is a character that can stand for something else - in the same way that the joker, or wildcard, in a pack of playing cards, can replace any other card. There are two common wildcards:

    @   stands for any single character
    ..   stands for any set of characters

So, if you want to find someone whose name you cannot quite recall, but is either 'Johnson', 'Johnstone', 'Johnston' or something similar, you could look for it with the expression:

    Johns..

Write that into the **Value** slot and set the **@ and ..** option, and Paradox will use the wildcards during its search.

The **Exact Match** option does not use wildcards - and as this makes the search a simpler process, it also makes it a faster one.

The **Advanced Pattern Match** uses an extended set of wildcards, and can be safely ignored for the time being.

When everything is set, click the OK button to run the search. Paradox will scan all the records in the file, stopping at the first match. To find any further matches, use the right-hand magnifying glass or the **Record|Locate Next** menu sequence.

17   Queries on a Single Table

Queries are crucial to database management, for they determine the nature of the information that you get from the database. A Query defines what you want, and the process of running a Query creates a new table containing selected data. The selection can be applied to records or fields or - more commonly - both.

At the simplest, a query will produce a table containing the items from certain fields only, but for every record in a file, or one containing a selected set of complete records. At the other extreme, the query will draw from several different - though related - files, taking only those records that meet a variety of criteria. The answer table will contain only certain fields and it will include calculated values, sub-totals and totals. We'll not attempt those just yet.

A query is an object, and like other major objects, such as tables and forms, it will occupy its own window on screen and can be saved as a file. This makes queries reusable - as they should be, for some will be wanted time and again. On a stock control system, you would do a weekly run to find items below reorder level; with a customer accounts database, you would perform a regular check for overdue invoices.

The results of the query are normally stored in a standard table named **Answer**, located in the directory defined by your PRIV alias. The answer table is intended to be temporary and will be overwritten by each subsequent query. Two points follow from this. If you want to keep the table for future reference, you must rename it before you run another query. Secondly, on a network, every user's PRIV directory must be different, or you will be overwriting each other's answers.

Queries on a Single Table 17

Defining a Query

Queries are defined by a process called **QBE** - Query By Example - and it is much easier than you might think at first sight.

1. From the menu bar select **File|New|Query**. The **Select File** dialog box will open.

2. Highlight the required file and click OK. If you can't see the file, use the Aliases or the Browser to change to the right directory.

Once the file is selected, the **Query Editor** window will open, and it will contain an **image** of the file to be queried. This image has the same layout and title line as a normal table, but with a little box in the leftmost column and in each field. These are **check boxes**. A tick in here indicates that the field is to be included in the answer table. The leftmost box is a special case - tick here if you want to include ALL the fields in the answer.

Selecting Fields

To select a field for inclusion in the answer table, click on its check box. A tick will appear as you do this.

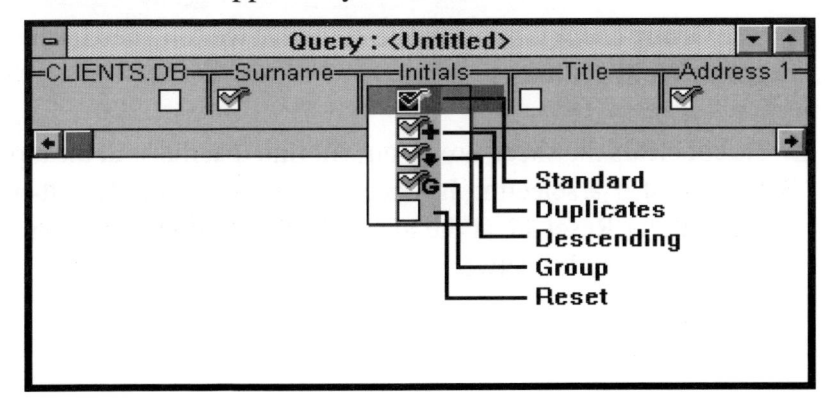

```
Query : <Untitled>
CLIENTS.DB   Surname   Initials   Title   Address 1
                                     ─── Standard
                                     ─── Duplicates
                                     ─── Descending
                                     ─── Group
                                     ─── Reset
```

83

17 Queries on a Single Table

If you are quick, you may notice a flash as a small panel appears and disappears. Hold the left button down on the check box to get a good look at this panel. It is a menu of icons that fine tune the selection.

Field Selection Modes

- The **Standard** check is what you get with a quick click. With this, the records in the Answer table will be listed in ascending order of the values in the leftmost fields, and duplicate records will be ignored.

- The **Plus** check includes duplicates. When Paradox is deciding whether or not records are duplicates, it looks only at those fields that are included in the Answer, not at the whole of the original records. Test this out later by setting up a query that includes just the Surname. Try it with a Standard check, and there will be only one Jones; with the Plus check, both the Jones will be listed.

- The **Down Arrow** sets the sort - on that field only - to descending. As Paradox will naturally sort the table in ascending order starting with the first field, this option won't have much effect unless it is used in the first or second field.

- The **Group** check raises complications that we don't need at this point. We'll get back to it later.

- **Reset** clears the check box. You will find that this is at the top of the list if a selection has been made in a field. As either Standard or Reset are at the top of the list, a simple click on a check box toggles between the two.

Queries on a Single Table 17

At the simplest, you might want to get a straight list of all your clients' names. Here is how you could get this:

1. First click on the check boxes in the Title, Initials and Surname fields to make the ticks appear.

2. Next, use the menu sequence **Query|Run** or the lightning icon to run the query. Paradox thinks for a brief moment then displays a new table, named **Answer**, and this one will contain name details for all the records in the file.

3. Scan the Answer table to make sure that you have got what you wanted. Did you include the right fields? Have you got as many records as you had expected?

That's all there is to it, and it has probably taken you a minute from start to finish!

18 Simple Record Selection

To produce an answer table that contains a particular set of records, you must define your selection criteria - the values that you are looking for. This may be items that are out of stock, customers who owe you money, or clients who are looking for a flat in the town centre. The selection process can be very sophisticated, but it is based on simple elements. You can look for exact matches, approximate matches or values above, below or within certain limits.

The selection criteria are written into the statement area - the space beside the check box - of the appropriate field (or fields). It's usually very straightforward - you just write what you are looking for.

Try out the examples below, using the sample CLIENTS file. Before you do each one, remove the previous selection criteria by clicking on its statement area and using [Backspace] to delete whatever is written there. Set the check boxes to display the Surnames and Initials all the time, for reference, then tick the box in the field on which the selection is based. (This is not essential, but it allows you to check that the selection has worked.) When the query is defined, run it with the lightning icon then view the results in the answer table.

Exact Matches

These work with text, numbers and dates. Just type what you are looking for in the statement area of the appropriate field. For instance, try "Newton" in **Town** and the answer table should show:

Surname	Initials	Town
Green	Teresa	Newton
Sergeant	Bill	Newton

Simple Record Selection   18

Likewise, try 2 in the **Bedrooms** field. You should find that Teresa Green and W.H.Smith are the ones looking for this size of house.

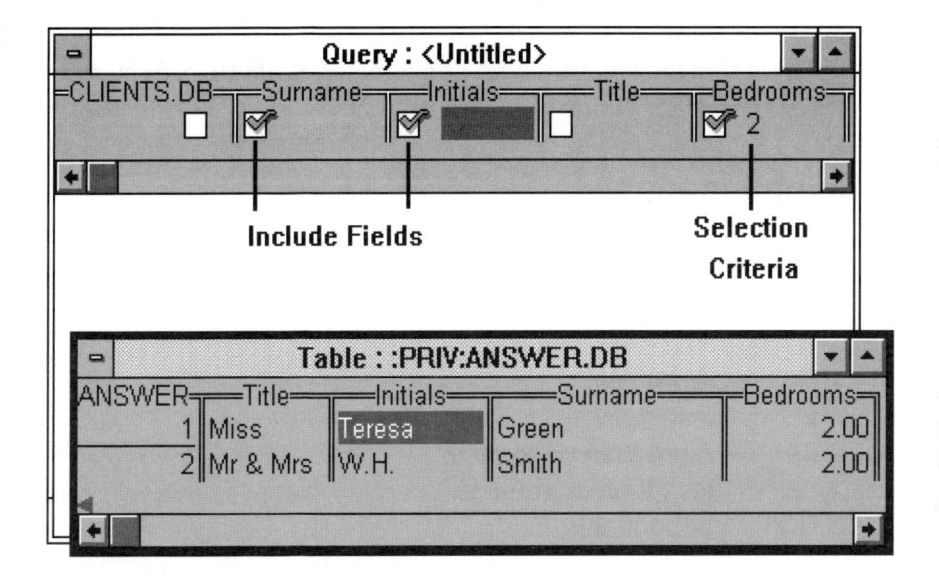

```
┌─────────────────────────────────────────────┐
│              Query : <Untitled>             │
│ CLIENTS.DB  Surname   Initials  Title  Bedrooms │
│     □        ☑         ☑        □      ☑ 2   │
└─────────────────────────────────────────────┘
           Include Fields            Selection
                                     Criteria

┌─────────────────────────────────────────────┐
│           Table : :PRIV:ANSWER.DB           │
│ ANSWER   Title      Initials   Surname  Bedrooms │
│    1    Miss        Teresa     Green      2.00 │
│    2    Mr & Mrs    W.H.       Smith      2.00 │
└─────────────────────────────────────────────┘
```

Approximate Matches

These only work with text items - but they are invaluable. There are two approaches:

■ The **LIKE** operator gives you a fuzzy search facility. If half or more of the letters are the same in the target and in the records, then that counts as a match. Type "LIKE Newton" in the Town field, and the answer table will contain D.J. Brown of Newtown as well as the Newton two.

■ **Wildcards** are symbols which can replace any given character or group of characters. They are the same here as in the Locate operations.

87

18 Simple Record Selection

The double dot **..** stands for a group. Try **N..** for the Town, and it will match 'Newton', 'Newtown' and 'Northampton'. Make that **..N..** and the selection will also include 'Old Newton'.

The at sign **@** stands for a single character. **Sm@th** in the Name field will find 'Smith' and 'Smyth'.

Comparisons

These use the relational operators and work with text, numbers or dates. The operators are:

>	more than
<	less than
>=	more than or equal to
<=	less than or equal to
NOT	not equal to

Who was looking for house under £100,000? Try **<100000** in the Max Price field. (Note that you must not write a comma into the number. It would confuse Paradox as commas have a special meaning here - see below.)

Where you want to include values that are on the boundary, use one of the combination signs. For example, , **>=4** in the Bedrooms field would find those wanting houses with 4 or more bedrooms.

When used with text values, the operators work on the ASCII codes. This is more or less the same as alphabetical order, except that all capitals come before any lower case letters. i.e. the sequence is A...Z then a...z. If digits are mixed in with them, as they might be in addresses, then numbers come before any letters. As an illustration,

Simple Record Selection   18

try <**M** in the Surname field, to pick out those clients in the first half of the alphabet.

Dates

Suppose you wanted to find those clients that you had not seen for a while. The criteria for the query would be that the Last Contact was, say, before 14th May. Paradox calculates happily with Dates, so the comparison operators < > = can be used here. The only small snag is that, in queries, Paradox needs dates in the US Month/Day/Year format. The expression in the Last Contact field would then be:

   <5/14/93

If you enter a date in the UK Day/Month/Year format and you will either get a '**Wrong expression**' error message or some unexpected results.

19 Selection with Multiple Criteria

When you want to narrow down the focus of your query, you can set criteria in several fields at once. Who was that chap from Newton that wanted a larger house? Write **Newton** in the Town field and **>3** in Bedrooms, and the query will find Mr Sergeant for you.

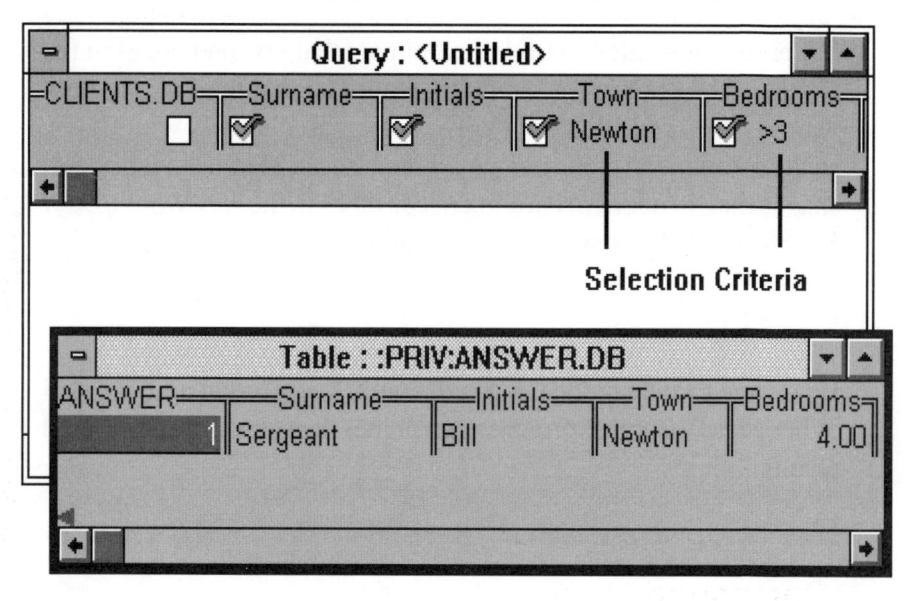

```
┌─────────────────── Query : <Untitled> ───────────────▼─▲─┐
│=CLIENTS.DB══╤═Surname═╤═Initials═╤═══Town════╤═Bedrooms═│
│      □      │   ☑     │    ☑     │ ☑ Newton  │  ☑ >3   │
```

Selection Criteria

```
┌────────────── Table : :PRIV:ANSWER.DB ──────────────▼─▲─┐
│ANSWER═══════╤═Surname═══╤═Initials═╤═Town═══╤═Bedrooms═│
│          1  │ Sergeant  │  Bill    │ Newton │    4.00  │
```

This is an **AND** type of query. Where the criteria are written along a single line, each of them must be true for a record to be selected. Sometimes you will want an **OR** type - where alternative criteria are acceptable.

Suppose you wanted to find those clients looking for either a larger house OR a more expensive one. The query would look something like the one shown below. You will see that it has two lines, with an alternative selection criteria in each. The check marks are identical in both lines - they must be there and they must be the same or the query won't work. (It's a pain having to go through the checking twice, but that's the way it is.)

Selection with Multiple Criteria   19

Checks in both lines   **Alternative Criteria**

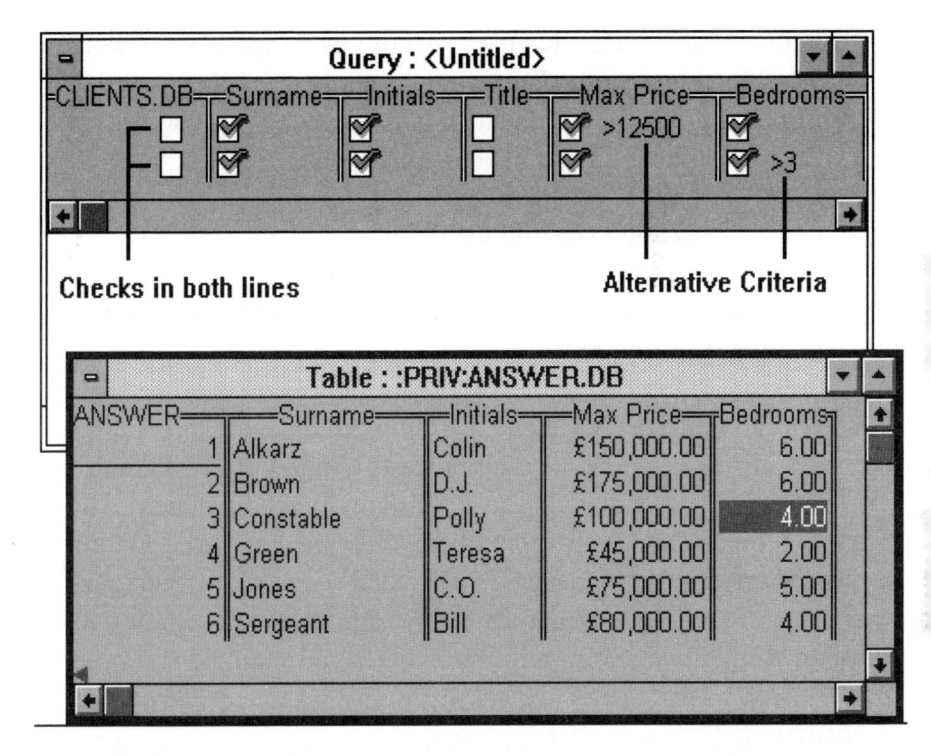

Compound Tests

You can also set multiple criteria within a field. Use these where you want to set alternatives or boundaries.

OR
Find the clients who are looking for middle-sized houses by writing **3 OR 4** in the Bedrooms field. This will then pick out those records with either value.

AND
Where you want to set two values that must both be true - as in fixing limits - you need the AND operator. For reasons best

19 Selection with Multiple Criteria

known to itself, Paradox uses the comma rather than the word AND for this operator. So, to find those who might be interested in a house in the £75,000 and £100,000 range, the statement in the Max Price field would be:

>=75000, <=100000

This translates as 'More than or equal to £75,000 AND less than or equal to £100,000'

You can combine the AND/OR operations to create single, complex tests, and you can combine multiple tests within fields with multi-field tests. You can do it, but I wouldn't really recommend it. The more sophisticated your logic, the greater the chance of getting tangled up in it. If you need to a particularly complex filter, a far better approach is to take it in stages. We don't have the sample data for anything truly complex, but take this trivial example.

Multiple Criteria by Stages

You are trying to remember the name of a client, either Jones or Smith, from Newton or Old Newton, looking for a smaller house. You could use these criteria:

Surname	'Jones or Smith'	
Town	'..Newton'	(.. makes Old optional)
Bedrooms	'>1,<4'	('2 OR 3' would work the same)

That would find Mr. Smith of Old Newton for you, but a typing error in any of the fields would ruin it - and you wouldn't necessarily realise that you had made the error. And with a more intricate query, logical errors are as likely as typing errors.

Selection with Multiple Criteria 19

Take it one step at a time - it may be a little slower, but you are more likely to get the right result.

1. Start by selecting the fields for inclusion, as usual.

2. Now write in the first criteria (here it would be 'Jones or Smith' in the Surname field) and run the query.

3. Scan the ANSWER table to check that you are getting all the Smith's and Jones's. If you are not getting the right set of names, correct the criteria and run the query again.

4 Add the second criteria ('..Newton' in the Town field) - in that same single line of the query. Run it again and scan the table to see who is left. Correct and rerun if necessary,.

5. Add further criteria as necessary to narrow down the focus, until the query find exactly what you are after.

Unless you have an extremely large file, searches are so fast that running the query a couple of extra times adds very little time to the whole process.

Saving the Query

You have struggled to work out the logic, and have finally got a query that finds exactly what you want. It would be a shame to have to go through the business again next time you want the same, or a very similar, set of records. Save the query. Next time, all you will have to do is open it, make any minor alterations that are necessary, and run it with a quick click.

93

19 Selection with Multiple Criteria

Save it as you would save a new table.

1. Select **File Save As..** from the menus.

2. Check the PATH - so that it goes in the right directory.

3. Type in a suitable, meaningful, name. Paradox will add the **.QBE** extension to identify it as a Query.

The Answer Table   20

Renaming the Table

The ANSWER table is temporary, so if you want to save it, you must rename it. Much of the time this serves no useful purpose. If you want a permanent record of the results, the answer table can be printed out as a report. If you have saved a query, you can generate a new answer table any time you want it. Sometimes you will need to save the table - to do further work on it later, to serve as the basis of a new datafile, or so that you can run other queries and then combine the results.

So how do we get these other names for the answer table? There are two ways. If the query has already been performed - so that the answer table exists - rename it.

1. Call up the menu sequence **Table|Rename**.

2. Change the path from PRIV to WORK (or wherever else you want to store it).

3. Type in the new name.

You can also define a name for the table before running the query. The answer table's name is then part of the query definition, and would be saved with it. If you ran the query again, the new output would overwrite the existing answer table - which may or may not be what you want. Try this approach anyway, partly so that you know how to do it, but also because it will get you into the **Answer Table Properties** menu, and there are a few other things there which you should look at.

95

20 The Answer Table

Answer Table Properties

When the Query Editor window is active, the top line **Properties** menu contains the entry **Answer Table**.

1. Select **Properties|Answer Table**, and then **Options**. The **Answer Table Properties** dialog box opens.

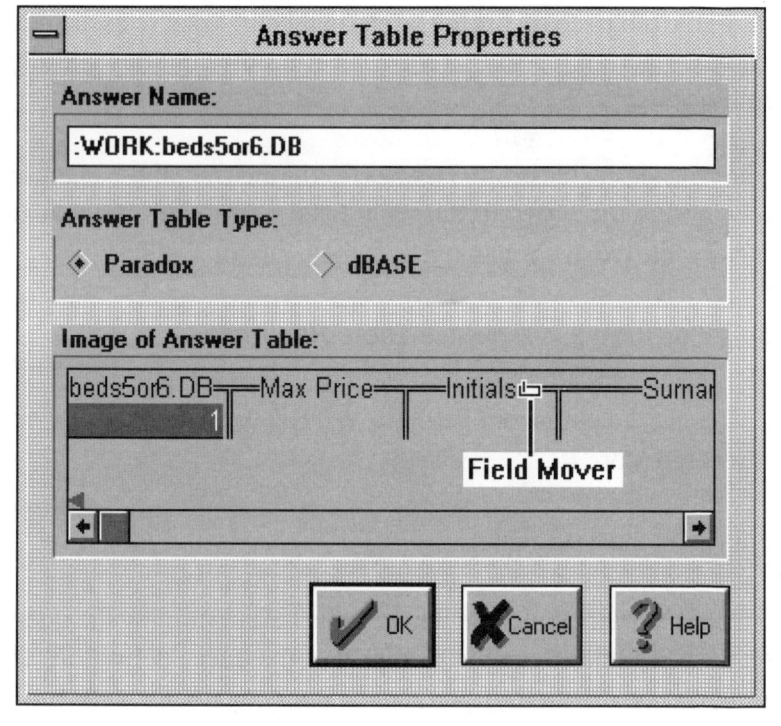

```
┌─────────────── Answer Table Properties ───────────────┐
│ Answer Name:                                          │
│ ┌───────────────────────────────────────────────────┐ │
│ │ :WORK:beds5or6.DB                                 │ │
│ └───────────────────────────────────────────────────┘ │
│ Answer Table Type:                                    │
│   ◆ Paradox        ◇ dBASE                           │
│                                                       │
│ Image of Answer Table:                                │
│ ┌───────────────────────────────────────────────────┐ │
│ │beds5or6.DB─┬─Max Price─┬─Initials┬─┬─────Surnal   │ │
│ │         1                                         │ │
│ │                        Field Mover                │ │
│ │ ←  ▮                                           →  │ │
│ └───────────────────────────────────────────────────┘ │
│                                                       │
│              ✓ OK      ✗ Cancel     ? Help           │
└───────────────────────────────────────────────────────┘
```

2. Edit the **Answer Name** to create a suitable name. This time you do not have a PATH option to give you a simple means of changing directories. So, if you do need to set a different path, it must be written into the name. If the target directory has an alias, its name must be enclosed in colons, e.g.:

    :WORK:beds5or6.db

The Answer Table   20

If there is no alias, write the full DOS path, e.g.:

C:\PDOXWIN\SALES\beds5or6.db

Even if you do not want to change the name, the Answer Table Properties are important because they allow you to set up the layout and style of the table - and those settings will be saved with the query.

- For those of you transferring data between different systems, the **Table type** options allow you to change the format of the resulting table. Obviously, if field types are not supported in the new format - like Graphics in dBase - data will be lost.

- If you want to change the appearance of the new table, move or resize the fields in the **Image** - the techniques are the same as with an ordinary Table. The Properties of the fields can also be set at this stage.

There's more to answer tables, and a lot more to queries than this, but we'll leave them for the time being. Our sample CLIENTS file is not really suitable for demonstrating calculations and the more complex queries. Also, we shall need a two-file system to explore interrelated queries. In the meantime, there are a number of other basic aspects of Paradox that should be introduced.

97

21 Sorting into Order

Where a table is indexed, it will be naturally sorted into the order of its key field(s). If you have worked through the earlier example, you will have noticed that after each new record is entered, Paradox pushes it into the right Surname/Initials order. In a table where no field is keyed, the records stay in the order in which they are entered. In either case, there will be times when you want to see the records in a different order. In a customer accounts file, you might well want to sort them into order by amount owing, so that all the big debtors are pulled to the top; a stock file might by sorted by type and name for a catalogue, or by bin number for stock-taking. It takes very little time to set up a sort, and even less for Paradox to perform it.

1. First open the table that you want to sort. If you are looking at the file as a form, select **Form|Table View** to access it as a table.

2. From the Menu bar select **Table|Sort**. Paradox opens up a window in which you will define the sort.

3. Decide where you want the sorted data. With a simple, unkeyed file, the sorted records can be written back into the **Same Table** or copied into a **New Table**. If the original is a keyed file, you have no choice. The keys establish a fixed order - the sorted records must be written to a new file. (Keyed files can be *viewed* in a different order. See below.) If you are working with the (keyed) example file, select **New Table** and call it 'Sortfile'.

4. Set the other two options as necessary.

■ **Sort Just Selected Fields** can be misunderstood. The sorting process will always move entire records - reordering a single field while leaving all the rest unchanged would destroy the

Sorting into Order 21

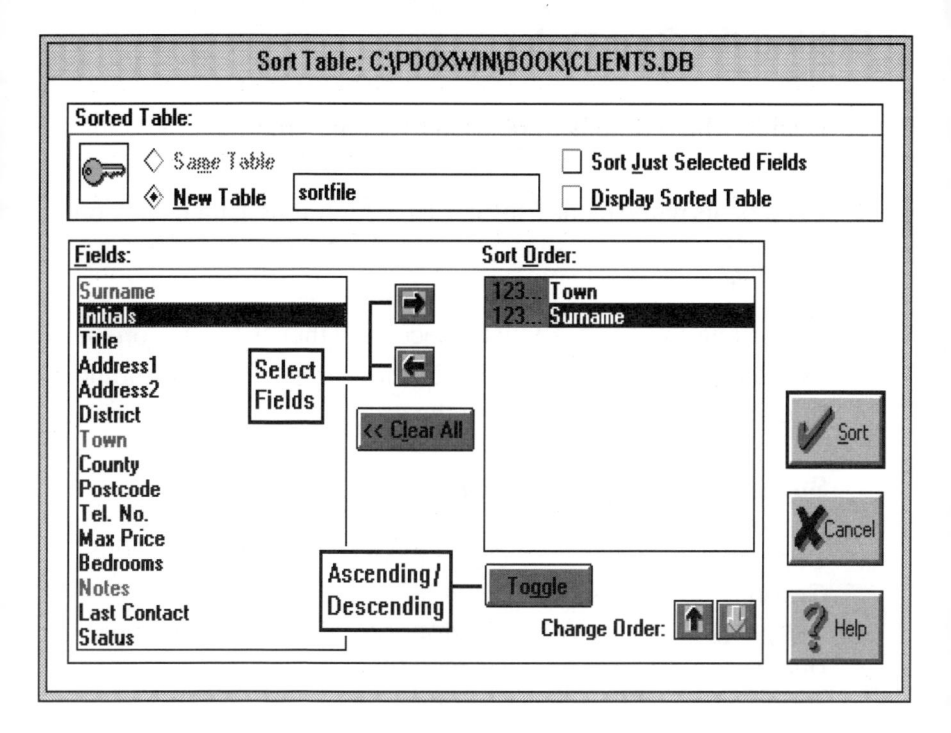

[Screenshot of Sort Table dialog: C:\PDOXWIN\BOOK\CLIENTS.DB, showing Sorted Table options (Same Table / New Table "sortfile"), Sort Just Selected Fields, Display Sorted Table, Fields list (Surname, Initials, Title, Address1, Address2, District, Town, County, Postcode, Tel. No., Max Price, Bedrooms, Notes, Last Contact, Status), Sort Order (Town, Surname), with Select Fields, Clear All, Ascending/Descending Toggle, Change Order, Sort, Cancel, Help buttons.]

integrity of the data. If this option is not set, the records are sorted first by the selected fields, and then in the order of the remaining - unselected - fields, working down through the list. For example, if we sorted the estate agents' file by town, then within each town set, the clients would be in order of their surnames and initials, as these are the first fields in the list. Set this option if you wish to override Paradox's natural inclination to organise.

■ **Display Sorted Table** only applies where a new table is being created. If this is not set you will have to open the file from the disk.

99

21 Sorting into Order

Setting the Sort Order

1. Decide which field is to be used to set the order.

2. Click on its name in the **Fields** List to highlight it, then click on the right selector arrow to add it to the **Sort Order** List.

3. With a one-field sort, all that's necessary then is to click on the **Sort** button. Try it using Town with the example file. You should find that the records will be in the order:

Surname	Initials	Town
Constable	Polly	Copsefield
Green	Teresa	Newton
Sergeant	Bill	Newton
Brown	D.J.	Newtown
Jones	C.O.	Northampton
.....		

Now try a multi-field sort. This time we'll order the records by number of bedrooms and maximum price.

1. Open the newly created Sortfile table, if it is not already on display, and select **Table|Sort**. As this is an unkeyed file, and as we have no reason to keep Sortfile in its present order, take the **Same Table** option.

2. Highlight the field name Max Price and click the right arrow to add it to the **Sort Order** List. Add Bedrooms to the list in the same way.

Sorting into Order 21

3. Use the Up or Down **Order Fields** arrows to position the names so that Bedrooms is on top.

Ascending or Descending

To the right of each name in the **Sort Order** List, you will see a green bar displaying '123...' This specifies ascending order. Double-click on the bar and it will change to '...321' on a red background. Double-click again to turn it back. A highlighted field can also be switched between ascending and descending order by clicking on the **Toggle** button - now there's a meaningful label!

4. Set both Bedrooms and Max Price for descending order, then click **Sort**. The records should then be ordered by number of bedrooms, and within that by price.

Surname	Initials	Bedrooms	Max Price
Alkarz	Colin	6	150,000
Jones	C.O.	5	75,000
Smith	A.B.	4	125,000
Constable	Polly	4	100,000
Sergeant	Bill	4	80,000
....			

101

- 3 -
Outputs from the Database

22 Reporting Out

In the next few sections we'll look at reports - the range of possibilities and how to produce them. In Paradox, a report can be a straight print out of what's on file. But it can be much more than this. Records can be grouped with sub-headings - and sub-totals; the selection and layout of fields is infinitely flexible; additional text and graphics can be added freely; and the report can be output to file or to any kind of stationery, including labels.

Quick Report

This is straight tabular printout of the data in a table, and could scarcely be easier.

Quick Report

1. Open the table for which you want the report - if it is already open, make sure that it is the topmost item on the Desktop.

2. Use the menu sequence **Table|Quick Report** or click on the Speedbar icon. Wait a moment and a new window opens, headed **Report: New**. This on-screen stage is your opportunity to check and possibly alter the design before committing the report to paper.

The layout is almost identical to that of a normal Table, with a few additions to make it suitable for output to paper. You will see the current date and the name of the file at the top of each page. With large records, the table will spread over two or more page widths.

Reporting Out   22

Surname	Initials	Title	Address 1
Alkarz	Colin		Station Road
Brown	D.J.	Ms	375 Long Lane
Constable	Polly	Mrs	49 Letsby Avenue

05 April 1993   CLIENTS

Report : New

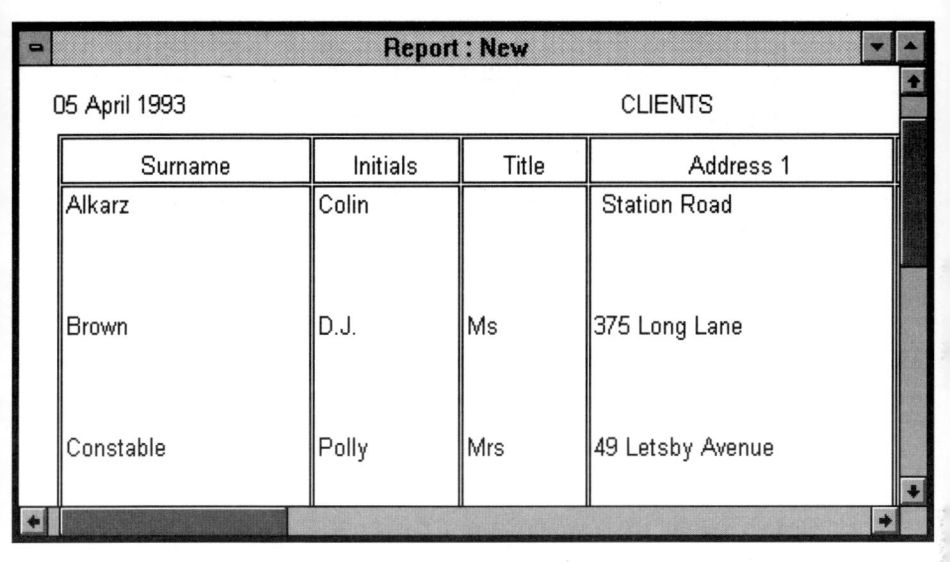

Scroll across the window, and you will probably find a broken line to indicate the right hand margin of the page. If the division falls in the middle of a column - and the chances are that it will - you have several choices. You can adjust the design now to make it fit better, or tackle the overflow at the print stage.

Assuming all is well, you can start the output process.

3. First, if you have access to several printers and do not want to use the default machine, use the menu command **File|Printer Setup** to select your printer.

Make sure the printer is on-line!

4. Click on the Printer icon or take the menu sequence **Report|Print**, and from the sub-menu either **Current Page** or **Report**, for a full printout.

105

22 Reporting Out

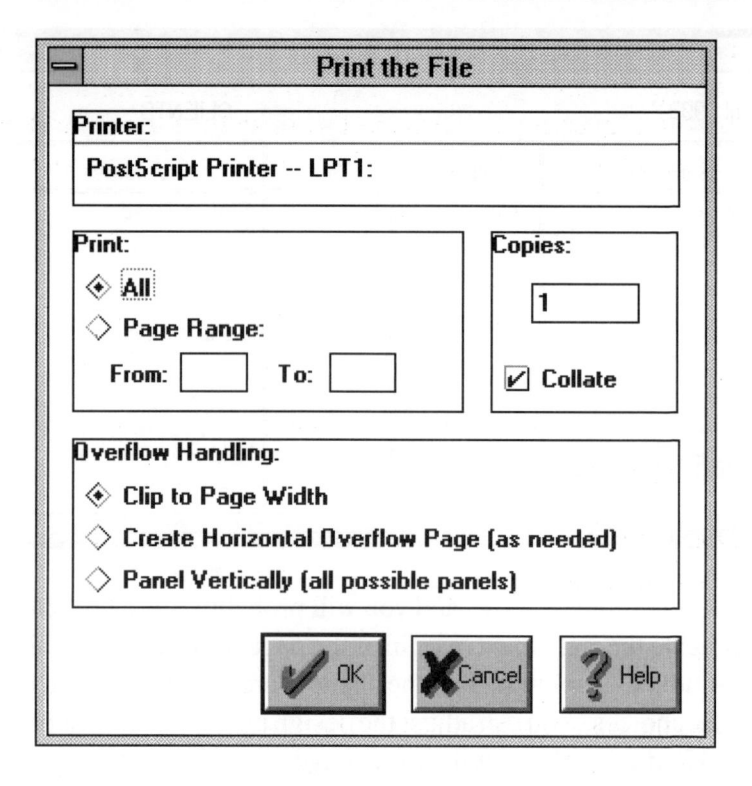

```
┌─────────────────────────────────────────────────┐
│ ▬              Print the File                   │
├─────────────────────────────────────────────────┤
│ Printer:                                        │
│ ┌─────────────────────────────────────────────┐ │
│ │ PostScript Printer -- LPT1:                 │ │
│ └─────────────────────────────────────────────┘ │
│ ┌─────────────────────┐  ┌────────────────────┐ │
│ │ Print:              │  │ Copies:            │ │
│ │  ◈ All              │  │  ┌───┐             │ │
│ │  ◇ Page Range:      │  │  │ 1 │             │ │
│ │  From: ▢   To: ▢    │  │  └───┘             │ │
│ │                     │  │  ☑ Collate         │ │
│ └─────────────────────┘  └────────────────────┘ │
│ ┌─────────────────────────────────────────────┐ │
│ │ Overflow Handling:                          │ │
│ │  ◈ Clip to Page Width                       │ │
│ │  ◇ Create Horizontal Overflow Page (as needed) │
│ │  ◇ Panel Vertically (all possible panels)   │ │
│ └─────────────────────────────────────────────┘ │
│         [✓ OK]   [✗ Cancel]   [? Help]          │
└─────────────────────────────────────────────────┘
```

5. When the **Print File** dialog box appears, set the options as necessary then click OK. The default settings will give you a single copy of all the pages in the report - i.e. all records - but only include as much of each as will fit across the page. In general, with a large record structure, you would be best asking for the horizontal overflow pages or vertical panelling, then get the Sellotape out and stick the pages together after printing. The CLIENTS table will have an overflow. Try each of the alternatives, and see what you think.

Quick reports go naturally with queries. They provide a permanent record of the results, without cluttering your disk; when defining the

Reporting Out 22

query, you will have included only those fields that are relevant at the time, so overflow and continuation pages will be less of a problem; and queries will largely be for use within the organisation, so that fine-tuning of the presentation is not a consideration.

Try it with the CLIENTS file.

1. Set up a query to give you a simple list of clients' names, their maximum price and number of bedrooms.

2. Check for inclusion the fields Title, Initials, Surname, Max Price and Bedrooms.

3. Don't bother with any selection criteria, unless you feel a desperate urge to practice.

4. Run the query.

5. With the answer table displayed on the top of the Desktop, call up the Quick Report dialog box and accept all the defaults with an OK. You should get a printout like this.

28 February 1993   ANSWER

Surname	Initials	Title	Max Price	Bedrooms
Alkarz	Colin		£150,000.00	6.00
Brown	D.J.	Ms	£175,000.00	6.00
Constable	Polly	Mrs	£100,000.00	4.00
Green	Teresa	Miss	£45,000.00	2.00
Jones	C.O.	Mr	£75,000.00	5.00
Jones	Peter	Mr & Mrs	£75,000.00	3.00
Sergeant	Bill	Mr	£80,000.00	4.00
Smith	W.H.	Mr & Mrs	£75,000.00	2.00
Smyth	A.B.	Mr	£125,000.00	4.00

23 Report Design

Reports are designed in much the same way as forms. You would normally use forms for the screen and reports for printouts, but you can print forms and view reports on screen. The key difference is probably that a form will always display only one record at a time, while a report page may contain a single record, a set laid out to your specifications or a table of records. Typical uses of reports range from simple printouts for reference, through mailing labels to summaries, valuations, catalogues and personalised letters.

You also have the same graphic design facilities that you have with Forms, and we'll come back to those shortly. First, let's tackle the more fundamental matter of getting the data into the report.

By way of example, we'll produce a summary of the clients file.

1. Select **File|New|Report** from the menus.

2. The **Data Model** dialog box will open. This is where you select the file. Click on the CLIENTS.DB filename. This will highlight it and post it across to the right side of the box. Click OK.

3. You will now see the **Design Layout** dialog box. This gives an overview of the layout and allows you to control the main features. The default setting is for a tabular layout with all fields labelled. We don't want the labels, nor the tabular layout.

4. Click on the **Single-Record** button in the **Style** box to select it, and on the **Labeled** button (just above the **Select Fields** bar) to remove the tick. You must set them in that order as the Labeled option is fixed in Tabular style.

Report Design

Single Record does not mean that you will have only one record per page - though you might do if they were very large records. It means that you will design the layout for a single record, and that layout will be repeated on each page as often as space permits. The name also distinguishes it from **Multi-record**, which we'll come back to in the next section.

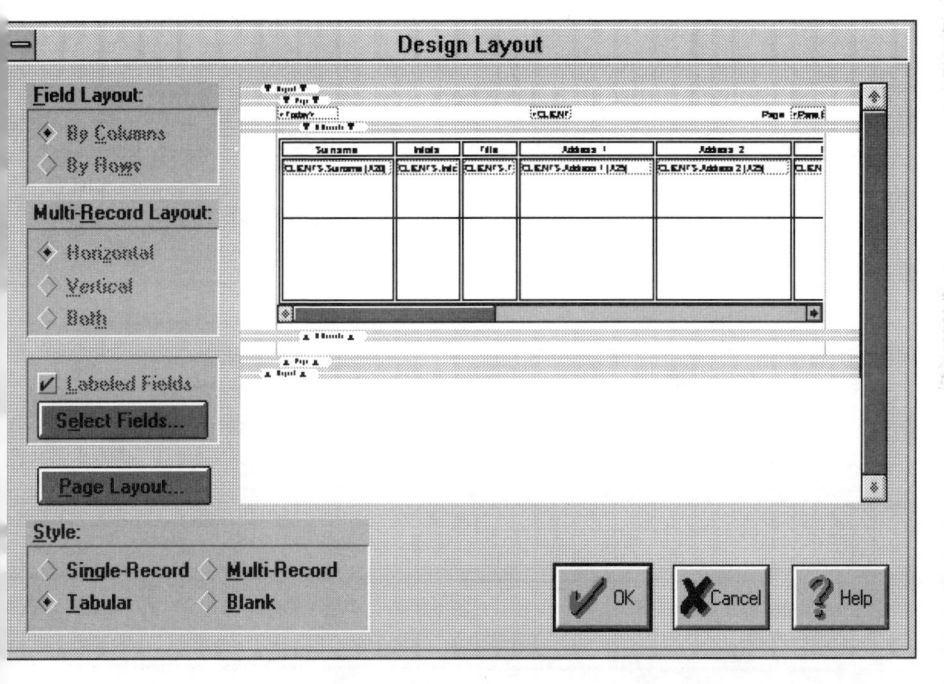

5. There are more fields in the table than we will want in the report. To remove them, click on the **Select Fields** button to open its dialog box. On the right hand side of the box you will see a list of the included fields - initially this will be all those in the table. Click on an unwanted field to highlight it, then click the **Remove Field** button beneath the list. Remove all the address fields in this way.

23 | Report Design

The **Order Fields** arrows allow you to move a highlighted field up or down the list. This can be useful, especially with tabular layouts, but it's not particularly relevant in this instance. We'll reposition fields at the next stage of the design process.

6. On the left side, you will see the name of the table with a button beside it. Click on this button and it will display a complete list of the fields in the table. Those that are included in the report are highlighted, those that have been removed are in plain text. If you've taken a field out by mistake, hold **[Ctrl]** and click on it in this list to bring it back in. (The **[Ctrl]** key is vital. Select a field without holding it down, and you will remove all the existing fields from the selected list!)

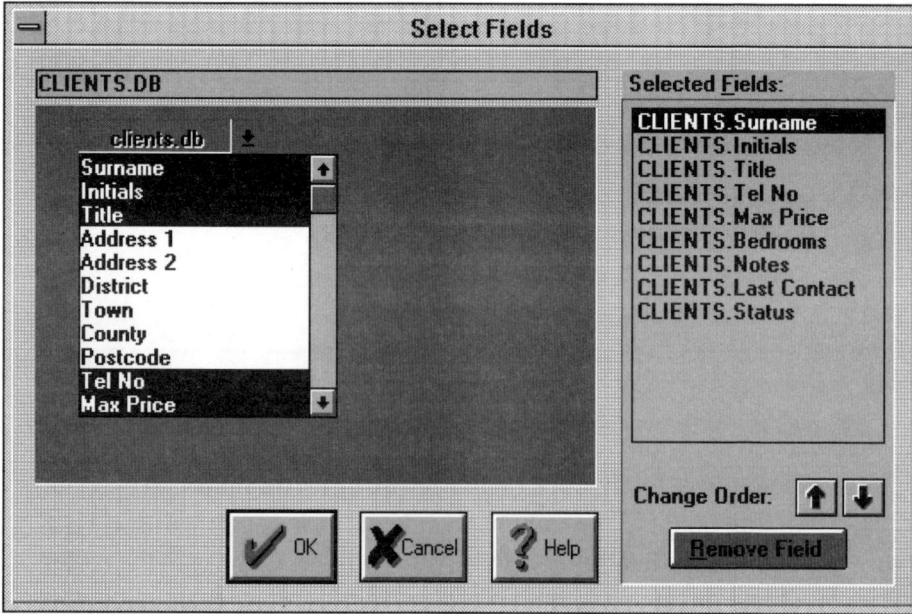

```
┌─────────────────────── Select Fields ───────────────────────┐
│ CLIENTS.DB                         Selected Fields:          │
│                                    CLIENTS.Surname           │
│   clients.db  ▼                    CLIENTS.Initials          │
│   Surname          ↑               CLIENTS.Title             │
│   Initials                         CLIENTS.Tel No            │
│   Title                            CLIENTS.Max Price         │
│   Address 1                        CLIENTS.Bedrooms          │
│   Address 2                        CLIENTS.Notes             │
│   District                         CLIENTS.Last Contact      │
│   Town                             CLIENTS.Status            │
│   County                                                     │
│   Postcode                                                   │
│   Tel No                                                     │
│   Max Price       ↓                                          │
│                                    Change Order:  ↑  ↓       │
│      ✓ OK    ✗ Cancel   ? Help        Remove Field           │
└──────────────────────────────────────────────────────────────┘
```

That should be all that's necessary now. (We'll come back to Page Layout in Section 25.) Click on OK to move to the next stage.

110

The Report Design Window   24

The Report Design window is where you will shuffle the fields into the right layout, add text and other enhancements and possibly arrange for the records to be grouped into categories.

You might like to start by setting the Properties for the Designer window. Select **Properties|Designer** to pull down the menu.

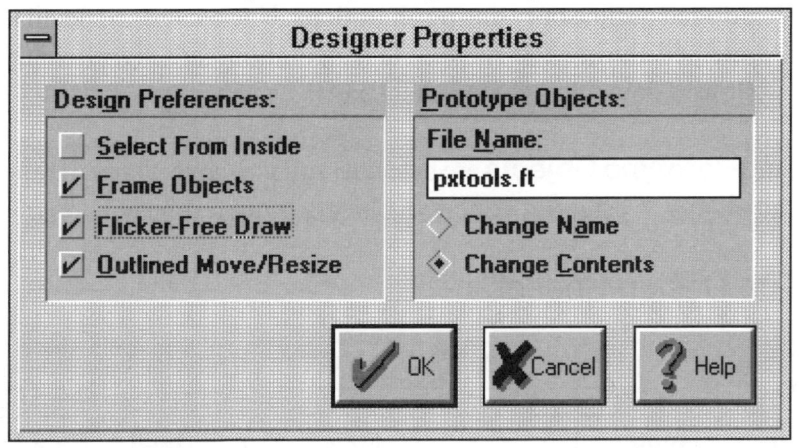

```
┌─────────────── Designer Properties ───────────────┐
│                                                    │
│  Design Preferences:      Prototype Objects:       │
│    ☐ Select From Inside     File Name:             │
│    ☑ Frame Objects          [pxtools.ft]           │
│    ☑ Flicker-Free Draw      ○ Change Name          │
│    ☑ Outlined Move/Resize   ◆ Change Contents      │
│                                                    │
│              [✓ OK]  [✗ Cancel]  [? Help]          │
└────────────────────────────────────────────────────┘
```

Design Preferences

■ With **Select from Inside** checked, you can select a Data or Label from within a Field area with a single click. Leave it unchecked and selecting inner objects takes a double-click - the first to get the overall Field, the second to get the Label or Data. If you are dealing with whole fields most of the time, it's may be simpler to leave this unchecked.

■ With **Frame Objects** checked, objects inside others - e.g. items in boxed outlines - are moved as a unit. With this unchecked, the box and its contents would have to be moved separately.

111

24 The Report Design Window

■ With **Flicker-Free Draw** checked, the screen update is smoother but slower. The more features you add to a report, the longer it takes to redraw the screen, and you may well decide that a few flickers are an acceptable price to pay for the improved speed.

■ With **Outlined Move/Resize** checked, objects are shown as a dotted outline only during alterations. Unchecked, all detail is retained during the move - and operations are significantly slowed down. Leave this checked.

The **Prototype Objects** are best left until you have plenty of time and energy. Designing your own objects is not for busy people.

The Design Speedbar

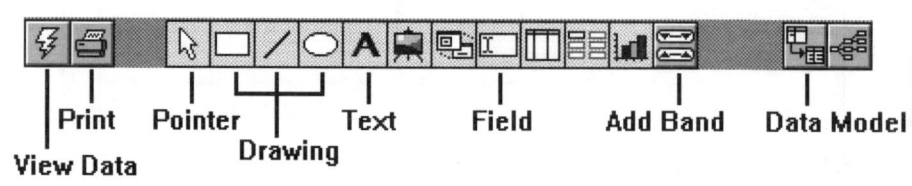

```
  Print   Pointer      Text      Field     Add Band   Data Model
View Data         Drawing
```

Your tools here are the same as in the Form Design window. Text, line, boxes, ellipses, graphics and fields are added in exactly the same way. The new icons are all on the right of the Speedbar. We'll tackle the rightmost one of these in the next section, and come back to the others later in the book.

Over on the left you will find the **Print** icon, which gives you one-click hard copy to replace the **File|Print** menu sequence.

The lightning icon is **View Data**, which provides a screen preview of the report. I find this invaluable for checking that data appears in the right place - placing fields is a fiddly business. All too often something that looks just right in the Design mode is out of line in the final layout.

Bands in Reports

A report is divided into bands, nested within each other. Fields, text and other enhancements can be positioned in any of these bands. The outer band is the report itself. Anything in the topmost band is printed once only, at the start of the report; likewise anything at the bottom is printed solely at the end.

Items in the top and bottom Page bands become the headers and footers on the printed pages. You will see in the screenshot that the top Page band includes the firm's name and the somewhat cryptic headings <Today>, <CLIENTS> and **Page <Page Number>**. These are added automatically to every report and will produce Today's date, the filename and the page number. If you do not want them, they can be removed.

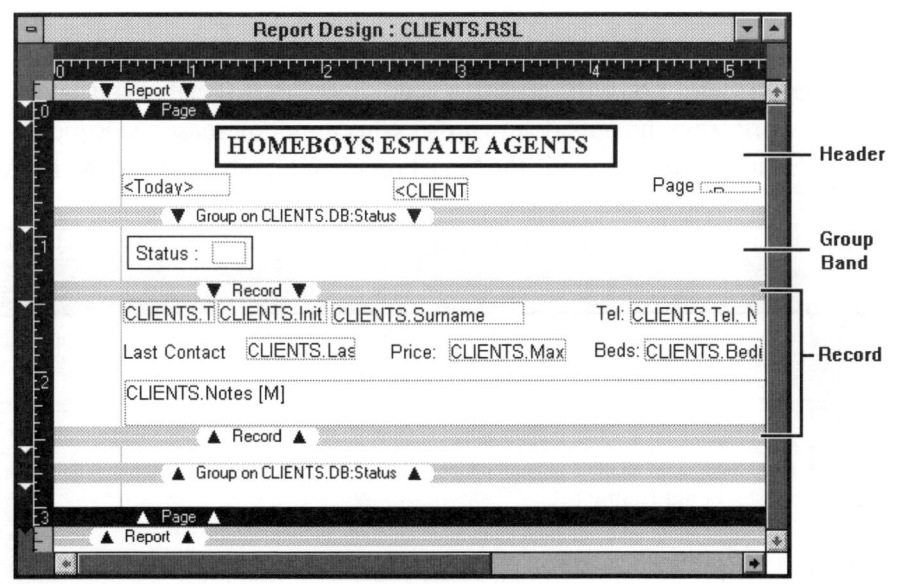

At the centre of the report is the Record band. This is where you determine the layout of the fields and those items of text or graphics that will accompany each record.

113

25 Bands in Reports

If you wish, you can add other levels of banding to sub-divide the report into categories. You will note on the example that the third band is labelled 'Group on CLIENTS.DB:Status', and that it carries the heading 'Status'. This will band together those records with the same value in the Status field. We'll come back to the mechanics of adding bands shortly.

When the report is output, Paradox will print several records per page, and as many pages as are necessary to include the whole file. How many records are on each page depends entirely upon the width of the bands for the records, groups (if any) and the header and footer. Band widths can be changed if necessary, though it needs some fairly precise mouse handling.

When you start, the bands will be just deep enough to hold the fields that go there. You will very often need space, and to get this you have to work from the outside inwards - you cannot increase the Report area until you have made the Page bigger. We'll start at the bottom.

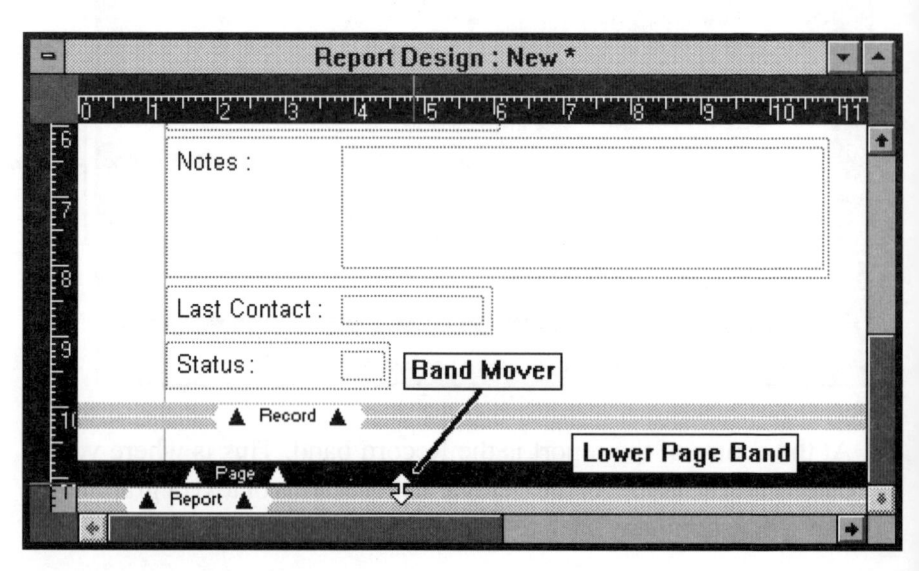

Bands in Reports

Stretching the Bands

1. Click somewhere on the upper or lower Page bands to highlight its borders. Move the pointer to the bottom band line and position it to get the double-headed arrow. There is a very narrow window of opportunity for this - pass the pointer slowly up and down over the band until the arrow appears.

2. Drag down. You should see a dotted line appear. Take this as far as you like - right off the page and out of the Report window if necessary. You will see a message in the Status line saying something like:

   Resizing #Page_Footer 21.00 by 2.35

   If you hit the bottom of the screen, and still haven't got enough depth, release the mouse button, let Paradox adjust the screen, then drag the band again.

3. You can now stretch the Report band in the same way. Click on the Report area to highlight the bands and drag the lower one down until you have enough depth.

4. Create space above the fields in the same way. Start by highlighting the top Page band and dragging it upwards, then highlight the Report band and drag its border up.

If you compare a screen preview with the printed output, you will find that Paradox is generous in its interpretation of width in the hard copy, so be prepared to shrink bands.

25 Bands in Reports

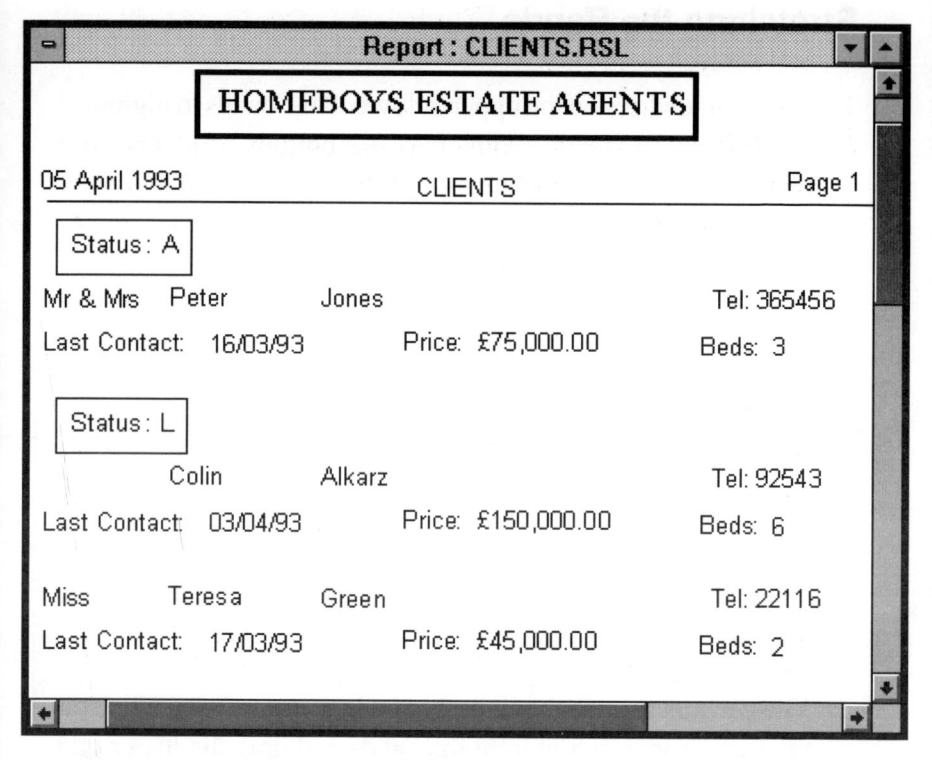

```
┌─────────────────────────────────────────────┐
│ ▫          Report: CLIENTS.RSL         ▼ ▲  │
│         ┌──────────────────────────┐        │
│         │  HOMEBOYS ESTATE AGENTS  │        │
│         └──────────────────────────┘        │
│ 05 April 1993          CLIENTS       Page 1 │
│   ┌──────────┐                              │
│   │Status: A │                              │
│   └──────────┘                              │
│ Mr & Mrs   Peter    Jones          Tel: 365456│
│ Last Contact:  16/03/93   Price: £75,000.00  Beds: 3│
│   ┌──────────┐                              │
│   │Status: L │                              │
│   └──────────┘                              │
│            Colin    Alkarz         Tel: 92543│
│ Last Contact:  03/04/93   Price: £150,000.00 Beds: 6│
│                                             │
│ Miss       Teresa   Green          Tel: 22116│
│ Last Contact:  17/03/93   Price: £45,000.00  Beds: 2│
└─────────────────────────────────────────────┘
```

If you find the thick, brightly coloured band divider lines a little distracting, pull down the **Properties** menu and turn off the **Band Labels** option. The dividers will then be simple thin black lines. In neither case are these dividers included in the screen preview or printout.

Grouping Records

Add Band allows you to group records together - typically by a field value, though there are other approaches.

1. Click on the icon to open the **Define Group** dialog box.

116

Bands in Reports 25

2. Click on the filename in the **Table** box and the list of fields will be displayed alongside.

3. Select the field - Status in this case - then click OK. When you look back at the report design, you will find a new band has been placed between the Page and Record bands.

4. Add a text label and the field to create sub-headings, and the band is ready for use.

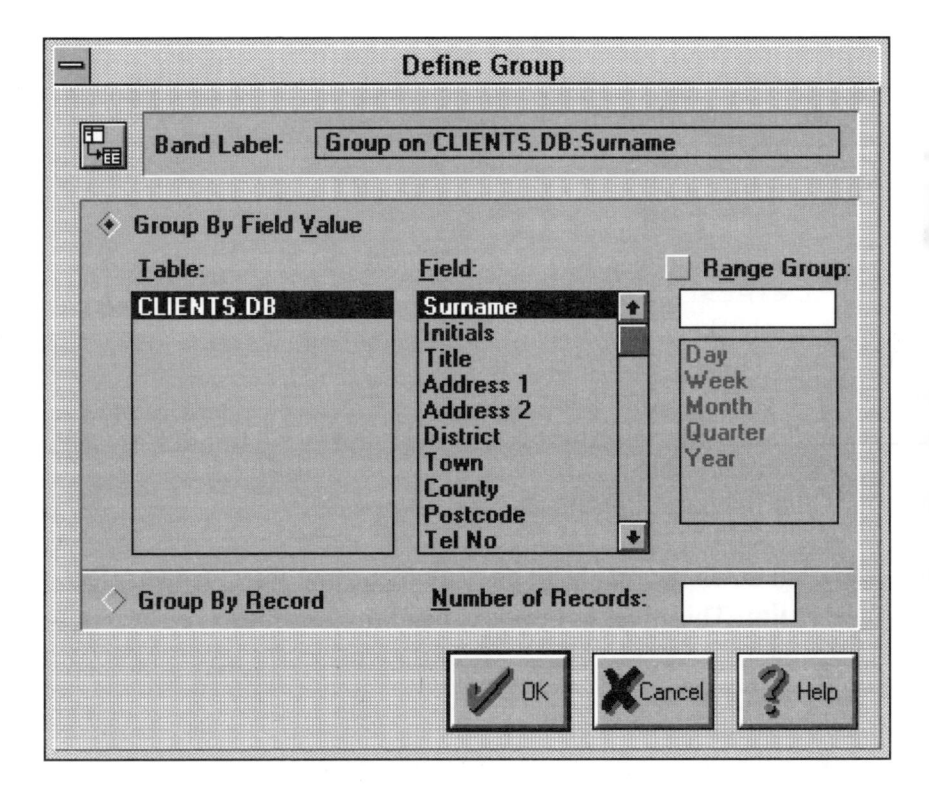

117

26 Report Design - Text

Small items of text are easily managed. You simply drag them into the right place and use their Properties menu to adjust the font and alignment. Once you get beyond a single line, it is time to look at the special text handling facilities. We can explore these now by adding a footnote to the report to explain the Status Codes.

First type in the raw text.

1. Expand the lower Page band, if necessary, so that you have room for 5 lines of text - 2 to 3 cms will do.

2. Click on the Text tool and use it to drag an outline 10cm by 2cm in the lower Page band.

3. Type this in:

   Status Codes:
   L <TAB>   Looking for a House   Press the [TAB] key.
   O <TAB>   Offer made
   A <TAB>   Offer Accepted
   C <TAB>   Completion
   Please check that the status codes for your clients are correct and up to date.
   Inform Mary of errors as soon as possible.

4. Pull down the main **Properties** menu and select **Expanded Ruler**. This gives us new text-handling facilities.

The Expanded Ruler

This appears as a band at the top of the Report Design window. Those tiny icons on it call up the main layout tools. To use any one of these, you must first select the text to which it will apply. If you

Report Design - Text

want the whole of a block of text, just click once on it - the handles on its outline show that it is selected. If you want part of the text within a block, double click, to get the text cursor, then drag highlights over the text that you want to format.

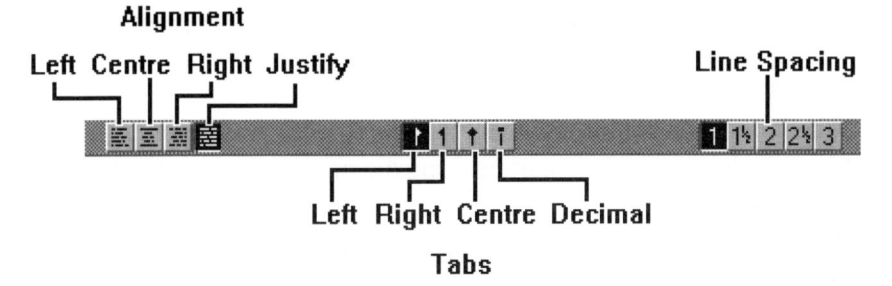

Alignment

Left Centre Right Justify — Line Spacing

Left Right Centre Decimal
Tabs

For the **Alignments** and **Line Spacing**, it is then a simple matter of clicking on the appropriate icon. Try them.

1. Select the whole Footnote and try it with the different alignments. You will probably agree that **Left** is the only one that works for the code lines.

2. Double click at the start of 'Please check..' to get the text cursor, and highlight these lines. Try a **Centre** alignment on these.

Tabs and **indents** are a bit trickier. For a start, these only apply to highlighted text or to the single line that currently has the text cursor. Secondly, the default tabs - set at 12.5cm (½ inch) - tend to stick around. In theory, those to the left should disappear when you place a new tabs. In practice, they reappear later. The problem seems to be that the tab settings are stored with each line, rather than the marked block. If you go back to the block later to adjust a tab position, the previous setting will still be retained by the individual lines. (I hope that this that will be sorted out in the next release, and in the meantime, try to get the tabs right first time.)

119

26   Report Design - Text

1. Use the text cursor to highlight the area in which you want to set tabs.

2. Click on the chosen tab icon, then click on the ruler to set the tab. Your new tab marker should appear, and the default tabs to its left should go.

The indent marker lurks at the left of the ruler. To move text in from the side drag the indent marker along the ruler to the required depth, then let go.

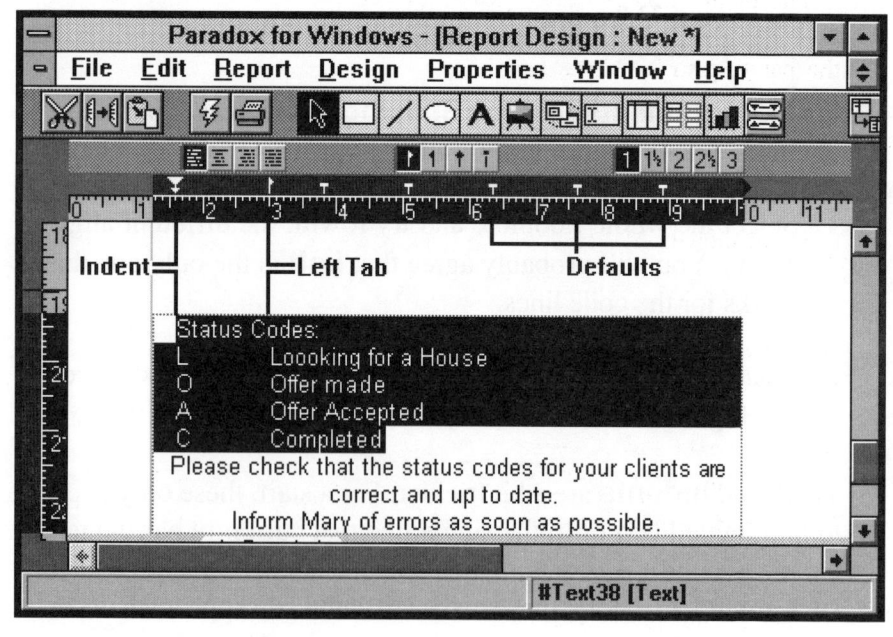

Paradox for DTP?

Paradox offers as much control over the appearance and layout of the page as some DTP packages. You can set the font, size, style and colour of text; add boxes, lines and circles in a range of line styles,

Report Design - Text

colours and fill patterns; and import scanned or painted graphics. The end results can be highly effective - but be warned, they should all be used with restraint. In the current version, these design features are not handled very efficiently by Paradox. In my early enthusiasm for the DTP facilities, I produced a personalised circular that with added text in a variety of styles and sizes, plus lines and shaded boxes. When sent to the printer it generated files of over 200k per page! An identical page (minus the data fields) produced through Pagemaker took less than 20k at print time. In these days of cheaper and more plentiful memory and disk space, we don't worry so much about size, but it's all relative. If I had tried to print all the records at once, the temporary print file would have been nearly 40 Megabytes! And size affects speed. The more memory it takes to represent an image, the longer it takes to process it, whether to send it to the printer or redraw the screen.

So, enjoy the facilities, but unless you are running a very fast and well-equipped machine, use them with restraint.

27 Mailing Labels

Though labels for mailings are probably the most common type, don't forget that you could equally well print price labels for products or identification tags for a stock system. All that distinguishes labels from other printouts is that there are lots of them on a sheet.

Some database systems have routines specifically designed to cope with labels. As far as Paradox is concerned, a label is just another type of report. There are both advantages and disadvantages to the Paradox approach. On the plus side, there's very little extra to learn, once you've mastered the report facilities, and there is great flexibility on layout and label sizes. Against that, the layout must be absolutely spot-on if the text is to hit all the labels properly. Expect to do several trial prints before you get it right.

1. Start as with any ordinary report. Give the command **File|New|Report** and select the Data Model.

2. At the **Design Layout** dialog box, select the **Multi-record** style. With the Multi-record options, select **Vertical** if you are using one-label wide rolls. Where there are two or more labels across the sheet, **Both** is what you need. The **Horizontal** option lays out the records across the sheet, but only one deep. There are very few labels for which this would be applicable.

3. Turn off the Labeled option, and run through the **Selected Fields** routine to trim off all bar the name and address fields. If you wanted to avoid unsightly gaps between the Title, Initials and Surname fields in the printout, then you would also remove those fields. The data can be brought back into the label as a calculated field. This time leave those fields in place. We will remove them and reorganise them in the next section.

Mailing Labels 27

Page Layout

This is concerned with the size of paper and the margins widths. I ignored this last time round, on the assumption that your page layout would have been correctly set at Windows level, and Paradox uses those settings. It won't necessarily be correct now, as the label paper may well be different.

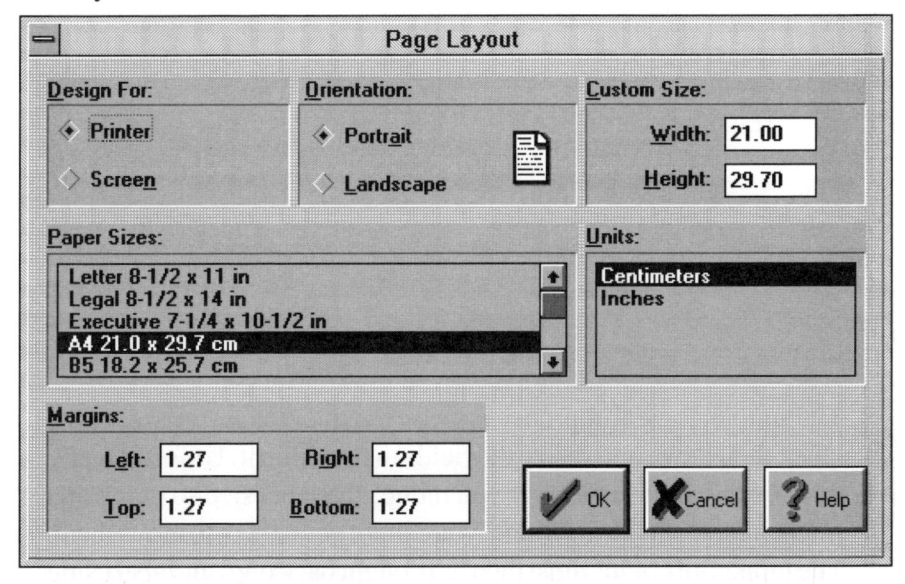

```
┌─────────────────────── Page Layout ───────────────────────┐
│ Design For:        Orientation:         Custom Size:       │
│  ◆ Printer          ◆ Portrait           Width:  21.00     │
│  ◇ Screen           ◇ Landscape          Height: 29.70     │
│                                                            │
│ Paper Sizes:                            Units:             │
│  Letter 8-1/2 x 11 in                    Centimeters       │
│  Legal 8-1/2 x 14 in                     Inches            │
│  Executive 7-1/4 x 10-1/2 in                               │
│  A4 21.0 x 29.7 cm                                         │
│  B5 18.2 x 25.7 cm                                         │
│                                                            │
│ Margins:                                                   │
│   Left:  1.27      Right:  1.27                            │
│   Top:   1.27      Bottom: 1.27    ✓ OK  ✗ Cancel  ? Help  │
└────────────────────────────────────────────────────────────┘
```

4. Click the **Page Layout** button. At the dialog box, select the appropriate paper size, if it is present in the options, or give the measurements in the **Custom Size** box. (Select either Inches or Centimetres for your measurements, using the **Units** option.) Set the margin widths to suit and exit with OK.

Designing the Layout

Now for the **Report Design** window. You will see that it is different this time, with one detailed label surrounded by shaded

123

27 Mailing Labels

copies. There are essentially two jobs here - design the layout of an individual label, and set the layout for the sheet. You must tackle the label first, as its size determines how many can fit on the sheet.

```
Report Design : LABELS.RSL
```
(Report design window showing label layout with fields: CLIENTS.I, CLIENTS.Surname, CLIENTS.Address1, CLIENTS.Address2, CLIENTS.Distri, CLIENTS.Town, CLIENTS.Count, CLIENTS. — and placeholders for Record 2, Record 4, Record 5.)

The simple, logical approach is to use the rulers to set the size of the label, then move and resize the fields to fit within it. Unfortunately, this doesn't always work. If you reduce the label size so much that fields are left outside its frame, you cannot get at them to move them. The lopped-off fields must then be brought back onto the label using the Field tool. I find that the job is best tackled in this order:

1. Do a rough positioning of the fields first - not worrying about any overlaps - so that they are all within the intended size of the label.

2. Highlight the frame by clicking anywhere within it and pull it into shape. Use the top and side rulers to get the exact size.

3. If fields overlap, reduce the Font Size so that they will fit across the available width. When doing this, remember that you can set

Mailing Labels 27

the Properties for several fields at once. Highlight the first field, then hold down [Shift] and click on the other fields. The handles will appear around them all. Now right click on one of the selected fields - any one will do. Set the Font size here, and it is done for all fields.

4. With suitable fonts set and the label size fixed, you can do a final repositioning of the fields before turning to the larger canvas of the sheet.

Right-click on the main body of the report to pull up the **Properties** menu and select **Record Layout**. This is where you specify the row/column layout of labels and the gaps between them. The defaults will be based upon the label size that you have set, with a guess at a suitable gap between them. Get your ruler out, measure your label sheet and correct as necessary.

```
                    Record Layout

                        Across      Down
        Number:         3           4
        Separation:     0.35        0.35

            ◆ Top-Down, Then Left-Right
            ◇ Left-Right, Then Top-Down

            [✓ OK]   [✗ Cancel]   [? Help]
```

5. Remove the Date, Title and Page Number fields from the top of the page. These rarely serve a purpose on label sheets.

| 27 | Mailing Labels |

6. Preview the report to see how it's going to look. You will see that the labels and the page have frames around them - these will be printed. If you don't want them, go back to the design mode, select the frames and delete them.

7. When you print for the first time, set it to print Page 1 only. There's a better than even chance that you've got one or other part of the layout wrong!

I find it's best to set the label size as smaller all round that the actual labels, with correspondingly larger gaps between them. This gives a little extra leeway at printing time.

8. Last thing - when you've got a layout that works, save it using the **File|Save As** sequence.

Combined Fields   28

If you store names, as we have done in the Clients file, as separate Title, Initials and Surname, it gives you more control over sorting, but it creates problems in the printouts. No matter how carefully you lay out the fields, no matter what properties you change, you cannot get separate fields to run neatly into one another if the size of the data items in those fields varies. You will finish up either with big gaps between the fields in some records, or overlaps in others - or both!

The solution is to use **Calculated Fields**. The fields that you add to your forms and reports are not limited to straightforward ones from the record structure. They can include a variety of calculations using number, special functions and the fields themselves. We'll get back to the numerical calculations and special functions in the third part of this book. At this point we'll use the facilities to join the separate Title, Initial and Surname fields into a single string of text. Here's how.

1. Go back to the Report Design window, if you are not already there.

2. Remove the Title, Initials and Surname fields.

3. Select the Field tool and use it to create a single box at the top of the label.

4. Select the Pointer tool and highlight the new field.

5. Right click to open its Properties menu and select **Define Field**, then pick ... from the top of the sub-menu.

6. The **Define Field Object** dialog box opens. Click the check box beside **Calculated**.

127

28 Combined Fields

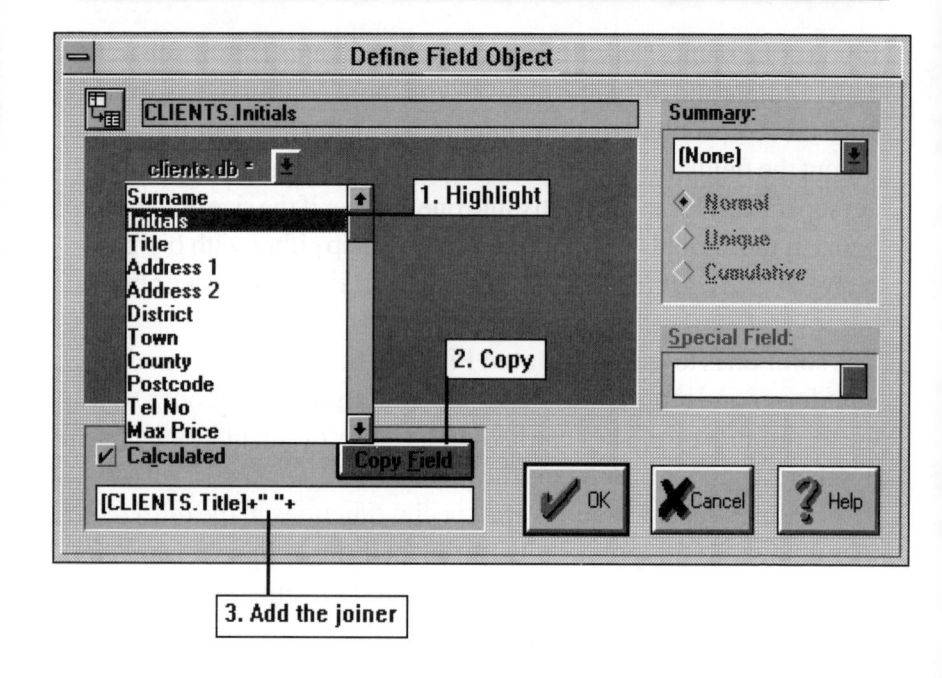

7. Click on the Filename slot to pull down the field list and highlight the first field to be joined - Title.

8. Click on **Copy Field** to transfer it to the slot at the bottom left of the box.

9. Click at the end of the field name to set the text cursor there. Type **+" "+**. The plus signs are the operators that will join separate items into a single string of text. The **" "** space in the middle is to stop the fields from running into each other. You want names in the form "Miss Teresa Green", not "MissTeresaGreen".

10. Repeat steps 7,8 and 9 for the Initials field, then 7 and 8 only for the Surname - that is the last item, so no joiner is needed.

Combined Fields   28

11.   Click on OK to end.

12.   Back in the Report Design window, get the Properties menu back for you new field and set the **Display Type** to **Unlabeled**.

Now try the screen preview or a printout and see the difference.

Personalised Circulars?

If you are producing mailing labels, you'll no doubt want a letter to go into the envelope. Experiment with the text-handling routines and calculated fields to create a personalised letter.

29 The Project Folder

There's an icon up on the right hand side of the Speedbar that I have been studiously ignoring so far. This is the **Open Project Folder** icon. It offers an alternative, and sometimes more convenient way of accessing your files. Click on the icon to open the folder.

The folder will normally display icons for the objects in your working directory. That doesn't mean that a folder is the same as a directory. Unlike a directory, it doesn't store files. All it holds are links to the files, which may be anywhere on the disks. It is the equivalent of a group window in the Windows Program Manager screen. There each window holds icons for a set of applications that are related by nature or usage, and this organisation cuts across the formal directory structure.

You need to be clear about the interrelation of folders and directories. Each directory contains only one folder, and it is the one in your current working directory that is available on the Desktop. If you use **File|Working Directory** to change that directory, it will bring a new folder to the Desktop.

Although initially the folder will hold all the objects in the working directory - and only those - you can add files from elsewhere, and remove those that are not wanted at the time. This is the main advantage of the folder. It gives you simple access to those files that you are using with your current project. You don't have to go browsing through the directories to find files - simply open the folder and pick the one you want.

As you can see, the folder can contain a mixture of file types. A directory can do the same, of course, but the normal **File|Open..** commands will only give you access to specific types of files. The folder can also remain open on the Desktop during your working

130

The Project Folder 29

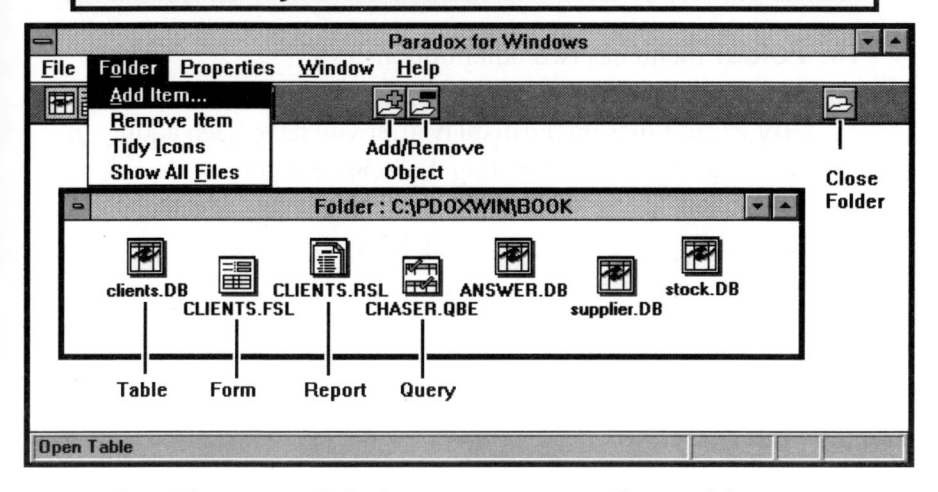

session. The net result is that you can open a form, table, report or whatever for your current project by a couple of mouse clicks - one to bring the folder to the foreground and one to open the file.

Adding and Removing Items

This is straightforward. To add a new item, click on the Plus icon, or use the menu sequence **Folder|Add Item**. This takes you to a Select File dialog box that is identical to those used during normal opening routines. Pick the file from the list if it is there - changing the <Type> if necessary. If it is in another directory, use the Browser to change to the right directory - and if it takes you a long time to track it down, just think, this is the last time you will have to struggle. Next time you want that file, it will be just two clicks away.

The **Folder|Remove Item** (or Minus icon) takes you to a similar dialog box, listing all the objects in the folder. Highlight the unwanted file and click OK to remove it. Note that this does NOT delete the file - merely its folder entry.

29 The Project Folder

The **Folder** menu has two other options:

Tidy Files tidies up the display after you have been adding or removing objects, or shuffling the icons around;

Show All Items is a toggle switch. When on it displays all the files in your working and private directories.

- 4 -
Relational Databases

30 A Stock Control System

It's time for some new sample files. There are some important features of queries and reports that we have not covered so far - largely because there was so much else to do, but also because the Clients file wasn't really suitable. We shall also be looking at relational databases - i.e. those that use several linked tables - and the new files are designed with that in mind.

This example could be the basis of a stock control system. It could produce stock valuations, lists of items for reordering, catalogues and bin or shelf labels.

There are two files - one for the stock items and one for the suppliers. They are linked by the supplier reference code that is present in both files, as 'SpRef' in one and 'Ref' in the other. Initially we will use them one at a time. Later we'll bring them together.

The data for the stock and suppliers' file are given below. These are for a DIY retailer. Add suitable addresses and phones numbers, and change the descriptions and names if you like. Leave the references and numbers as they are as they have been carefully structured for use in later examples. The field types, and suitable sizes for the Alphabetic fields are given beneath the headings. ('Qty' = Quantity in Stock; 'Reord' = Reorder Level.)

Key Fields

In these tables, the fields 'Ref' in Stock and 'SpRef' in Supplier must be defined as key fields. Do this when creating the tables by moving the cursor into the **Key** column and pressing the spacebar. An asterisk will appear to mark the field as a key.

A Stock Control System 30

A couple of things follow on from the use of key fields. First, the data in those fields must be unique. Some fields are therefore not suitable for use as keys. In the Stock file given here, for instance, neither the 'Category' nor 'SpRef' could serve as keys as they both contain repetitions. This uniqueness requirement provides an automatic check against accidental repetition. Try typing in two records with identical reference codes, and you will get the message **Key violation**.

Stock File

Ref	Description	Pack	Type	SpRef	Cost	Qty	Reord	Retail
A 5*	A 30	A 6	A 6	A 3	$	N	N	$
FC203	Ceramic Tiles - Marble 30x30	9	Floor	ICL	£9.23	120	50	£14.99
FC214	Ceramic Tiles - Grey 30x30	9	Floor	ICL	£8.79	60	50	£14.49
FW501	Hardwood Flooring - Ash	1sq m	Floor	WPI	£17.45	20	10	£23.99
FW502	Hardwood Flooring - Beech	1sq m	Floor	WPI	£17.45	8	10	£23.99
WP309	Wallpaper - Woodchip -11yd	5	Wall	WPI	£0.95	72	100	£1.49
WP313	Wallpaper - Embossed - 18yd	5	Wall	IDU	£1.45	40	30	£2.25
WT207	Tiles - Grey/Floral 11x11cm	9	Wall	ICL	£13.26	40	25	£16.99
WT411	Tiles - Black Diamond 20x20	9	Wall	CPS	£15.85	15	25	£18.49
WW709	Cladding, T & G - 1800x10 cm	6	Wall	WPI	£4.89	24	20	£6.99
WW712	Shiplap Cladding - 1800x10cm	6	Wall	WPI	£4.05	8	10	£5.99

Supplier File

SpRef	Name	Address1	Address2	Tel
A 3*	A 30	A 30	A 30	A 15
CPS	Cotswold Potteries		DIY!	
ICL	Italian Ceramics			
IDU	Interior Designs Unlimited			
WPI	Wood Products International			

135

31 Friendlier Forms

These new files offer a good opportunity to explore a little deeper into Form design. In this section we'll make use of the Quick Form facility again, but also go through the fuller New Form process, and introduce three new display types.

We could use two forms with the Stock file. One will include all fields and will be used for entering new items and for editing those values that are more or less constant - e.g. the Description, Supplier Reference, Reorder Level, Cost and Retail prices. The second form will carry only the Reference, Description, Pack size and Quantity in stock. This is sufficient for the regular updates of the quantity in stock, and as it has no sensitive data, could be used in the presence of a client to check the availability of an item.

Start the first form with the Quick Form facility, then when you've got it on the Desktop, switch into Design mode. We're going to make full use of the Display Types here to make this more user-friendly.

Values by Selection

Where a field will only ever contain one of a limited number of values, the alternatives can be written into the Form design. The user can then simply select the appropriate value. This doesn't just save typing time, it also eliminates the possibility of entering anything other than a correct value. In the Stock file, for instance, the Type might be one of 'Floor', 'Wall', 'Paint', 'Timber'. The SpRef will likewise have only a limited set of possible values.

Paradox offers three ways of handling this situation. If you highlight a field and pull down the **Properties|Display Type** menu, you will see the headings **'Dropdown Edit'**, **'List'** and **'Radio**

Friendlier Forms 31

Buttons'. They will each will hold a set of alternative values, though the method of selection varies.

■ With a **List**, you select by highlighting the value.
■ With **Radio Buttons**, you click on the diamond beside your choice.
■ With **Dropdown Edit,** you can select as from a List, or type in a new value.

Apart from the type-in option of Dropdown Edit, there is little practical difference between them. The choice is there mainly to provide a little variety in your forms.

Dropdown Edit   **List** 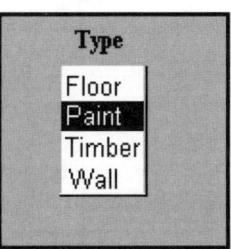   **Radio Button**

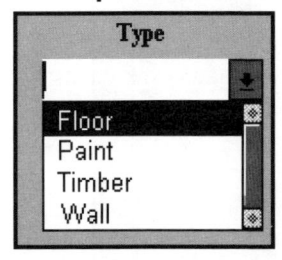

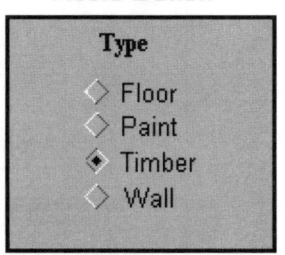

Creating a List

These three are all set up in the same way.

1. Right click on the field to get the **Properties** menu and select **Display Type**. That will take you to the **Define List** dialog box.

2. Type the alternative values into the **Item** slot, pressing [Enter] after each. They will be copied into the **Item List** in the order in which they are entered.

137

31 Friendlier Forms

3. If you want them in alphabetical order, use the **Sort List** utility after you have entered them all.

4. If you have made any errors, highlight the faulty item and either **Remove** it or use **Modify Item** to pull it back into the entry slot for editing. A highlighted item may also be moved up or down the list with the **Change Order** arrows.

5. Click on **OK** to get back to the Form Design window.

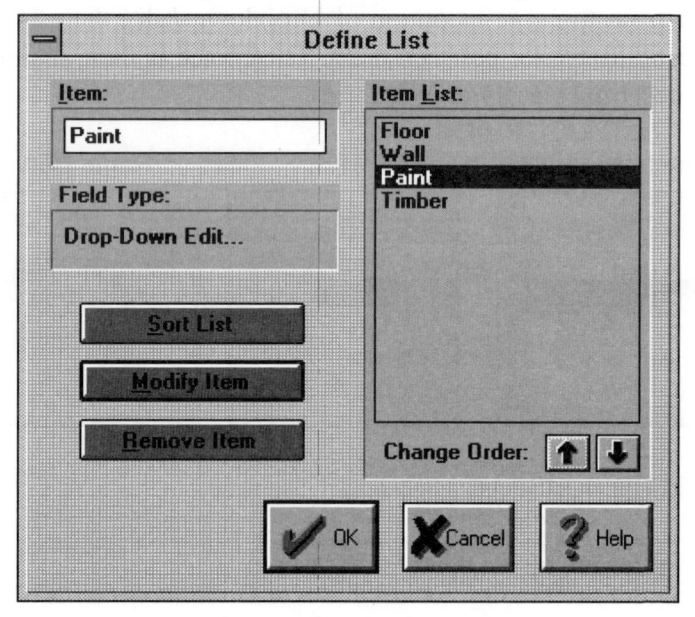

There is the same long-term flexibility here as elsewhere in the Paradox system. So, while it is a good idea to get things right from the start, there's nothing to stop you editing the list or changing its display type at any time in the future, when the database is in use.

Try these display types now with the Category field and the Supplier Reference.

Query by Example   32

Back in Section 17 we covered the basics of creating and running queries - how to select fields and to find records that match given criteria. In this section we'll put the Example into 'Query By Example'. Examples are used to create links between fields - either in the same table, or in linked tables.

We are going to set up a query that will find those items that need reordering. To find them, Paradox will have to compare the contents of two fields - Quantity and Reorder Level. Open a New Query and select the Stock file. Click on the leftmost check box - we may as well include all the fields in the answer.

Example Elements

An example element has no specific value. When written into a field it tells Paradox to look at the contents of that field in each record, when the query is run. The example itself is simply an identifier - a name. These can be real words or values - they don't have to be meaningful, but it helps if they are easy to remember. Though they are called 'examples', they need have no resemblance whatsoever to the data in the fields. You could even use the same word for the example as for the field name - there would be no conflict. So, an example in the 'Type' field could be *'Type'*, *'Floor'* or *'XYZ'*. Those of you who have done any programming will no doubt recognise that we are dealing here with variables, and variables can have any name you like to give them. The only real restrictions on the examples are that each must be a single word and that, in any one query, each much be unique.

Let's try them out. Once you have done the first couple, you'll find that they are easy to set up and simple to use. We'll create an example called *'level'* in the Reorder field, and use that to test whether any items have Quantity values below the reorder level.

139

32　　　　　　　　　　Query by Example

1. Click on the statement area in the Reorder Level field.

2. Press **[F5]** and type '*level*' - it should appear in red. If it is written in black, delete it, press [F5] and try again. The only possible problem that you will have here is in the [F5] keypress. There's no way of telling that you are in 'example typing' mode, and [F5] is a toggle switch. Press it twice (and a heavy keypress can register as a double press) and it switches back to ordinary typing mode.

3. Move to the statement area of the Quantity field. You want a test here that says 'less than the value in the Reorder field.' For this you need the '<' comparison operator and the 'level' example. Create the expression with this sequence:

   1) Type '<' as normal, so that it appears in black;
   2) Press [F5]
   3) Type 'level' - it should appear in red.

Your query should look something like this - except that you will have red characters instead of the italics shown here.

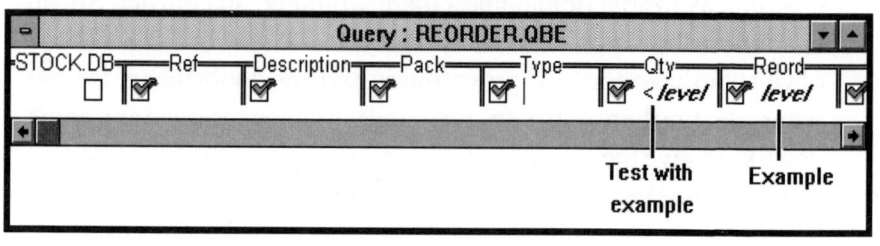

STOCK.DB	Ref	Description	Pack	Type	Qty	Reord
☐	☑	☑	☑	☑	☑ <*level*	☑ *level*

　　　　　　　　　　　　　　　　Test with　　Example
　　　　　　　　　　　　　　　　example

4. That's it! You have made the link. When the query is run, Paradox will compare the Quantity and the Reorder Level fields in each record, and select those where the Quantity is less. Run it and check the two values in the records thrown up by the query.

140

Queries in Linked Tables 33

The most surprising thing about working with multiple tables in Paradox is how easy it is. Relational database work has something of an air of 'experts only' about it, probably because earlier relational database management software really was for experts only. Forget that. Paradox makes it so simple - once you have mastered the art of using examples.

As an illustration, we'll extend the existing Reorder query to pull in the suppliers' names and addresses from the other file.

1. Return to the Query window and select the Plus icon, or the menu sequence **Query|Add Table**. Select the Supplier table from the list. You will now have images of both tables in the Query window.

2. Set the check boxes in Supplier here to include the names and addresses. The reference code can be left unchecked as we already have it from the other table.

3. Go to the SpRef field of the Stock table. Press [F5] and write '*ABC*' or something similarly suitable. Go to the Ref field of the Supplier table, press [F5] and write exactly the same example there. Your query should look like this - except with red lettering instead of italics.

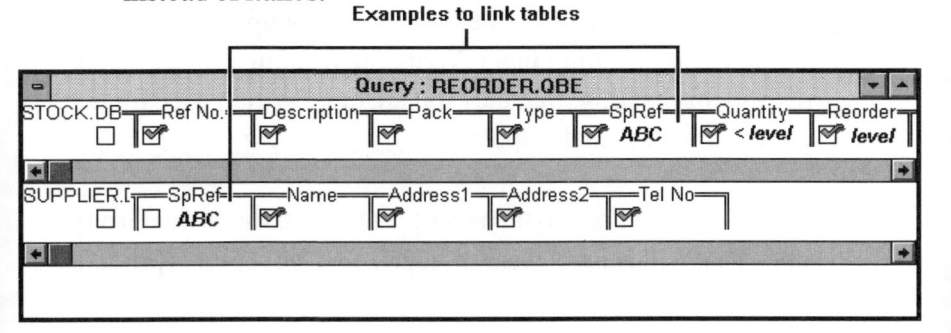

Examples to link tables

STOCK.DB	Ref No.	Description	Pack	Type	SpRef ABC	Quantity < level	Reorder level

SUPPLIER.[	SpRef ABC	Name	Address1	Address2	Tel No

141

33   Queries in Linked Tables

No further work is needed. When you run the query, each time Paradox selects a record from the Stock table, it will look up the matching SpRef in the Supplier table and copy the selected fields from both into the answer. There's likely to be repetition in here, of course. If the query finds ten items from the same supplier, that supplier's data will be included ten times. This must be borne in mind when organising a printout from the answer table. A Quick Report would include that repetition, and printing that would be a waste of time and paper. Instead the report should be designed from scratch, with the items grouped by supplier and each supplier's details written once only in the group heading.

1. Select **File|New|Report**

2. At the Design Layout stage, select **Single Record** mode, with fields placed Left to Right and unlabeled. The **Selected Fields** should be only those directly relating to the stock items - Ref, Description, Pack, Type, Quantity and Reorder Level. Supplier's details should NOT be included.

3. In the Report Design window, add a band to group on SpRef (or Supplier Name - the effect would be the same). Stretch it to give room for two lines of text.

4. Use the Field tool to place the fields for the supplier's details in the top Group heading band. Write the headings for the stock fields in this band, so that they too are only written once for the set of items from each supplier.

5. Add two drawn lines to the report. Put one in the lower Group band. That will act as a clear divider when the report is printed.

Queries in Linked Tables 33

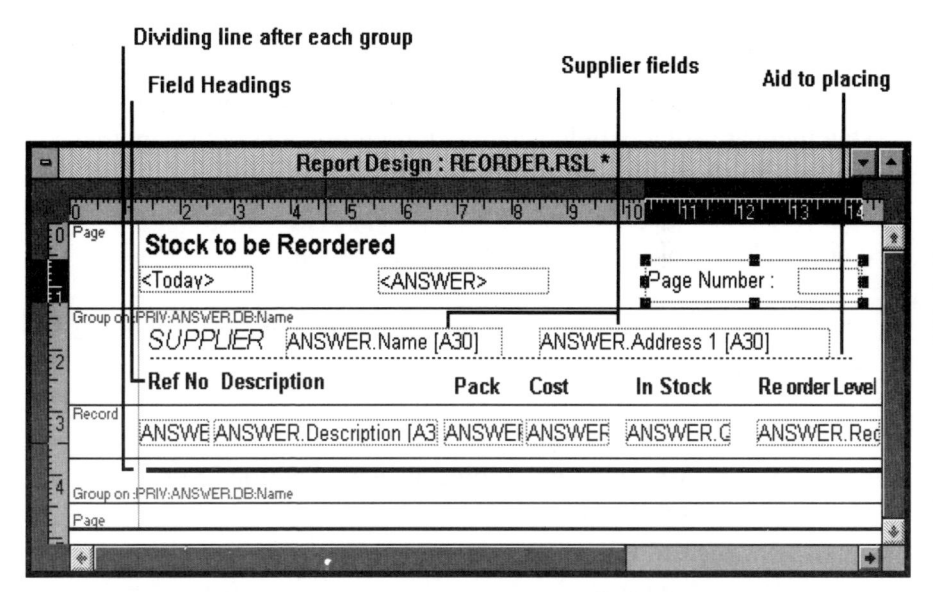

Screenshot of Report Design: REORDER.RSL with annotations:
- Dividing line after each group
- Field Headings
- Supplier fields
- Aid to placing

Design contains: "Stock to be Reordered", `<Today>`, `<ANSWER>`, "Page Number:", SUPPLIER ANSWER.Name [A30], ANSWER.Address 1 [A30], and the column headings Ref No, Description, Pack, Cost, In Stock, Re order Level with ANSWER field placeholders.

Draw a second, thinnner line in the top Group band. The main purpose of this is not to underline the supplier details, but to provide a guide for placing the fields. It is very difficult to place anything accurately by eye, but quite simple with a guide line. If you don't want the line in the printed output, it can be deleted once the fields are in position.

Sample report output (REORDER.RSL):

Stock to be Reordered
8 April 1993   ANSWER   Page Number: 1

SUPPLIER Cotswold Potteries

Ref No	Description	Pack	Cost	In Stock	Reorder Level
WT411	Tiles - Black Diamond 20x20cm	9	£15.85	15	25

SUPPLIER Wood Products International

Ref No	Description	Pack	Cost	In Stock	Reorder Level
FW502	Hardwood Flooring - Beech	1 sq m	£17.45	8	10

143

34   Calculations in Queries

Queries may contain calculations. These will consist of the reserved word **CALC** and an expression made up of actual values and example field references. A calculation may be written into the statement area of any field, whether it is empty or contains another expression, and whether or not that field plays any part in the calculation. When the answer table is produced, Paradox will create a new field to hold the results of the calculation.

The calculations are restricted to those using the standard arithmetic operators, which should be all you need for most business purposes.

Operator	Meaning
+	Addition (and joining strings - Section 28)
-	Subtraction
*	Multiplication
/	Division

The normal priorities apply. If a calculation contains a mixture of signs, the multiplication and division operations are done before the addition and subtraction. Enclose an operation in brackets if you want that part of the expression to be calculated first. e.g.

    2 + 3 * 4   = 2 + 12 = 14
    (2 + 3)* 4   = 5 * 4 = 20

CALC

Suppose you wanted to find the VAT on the retail price of the items in your stock file. Here is how you would do this.

1. Create an example in the Retail field - call it *'Price'*. Type in a comma then the expression:

CALC Price * 17.5/100

Calculations in Queries 34

Don't forget to press [F5] each time, before you write *'price'*. If it is not red, it is not an example.

2. Run the query.

3. Look in the answer table and you should find a new field headed **Retail * 17.5/100**. In that field you will find the VAT due on each item.

That's all there is to it! As long as you remember to press [F5] before typing an example, you can hardly go wrong.

Check your screen. It should look like the screen shot here - except that I have shrunk the columns to squeeze them on the page.

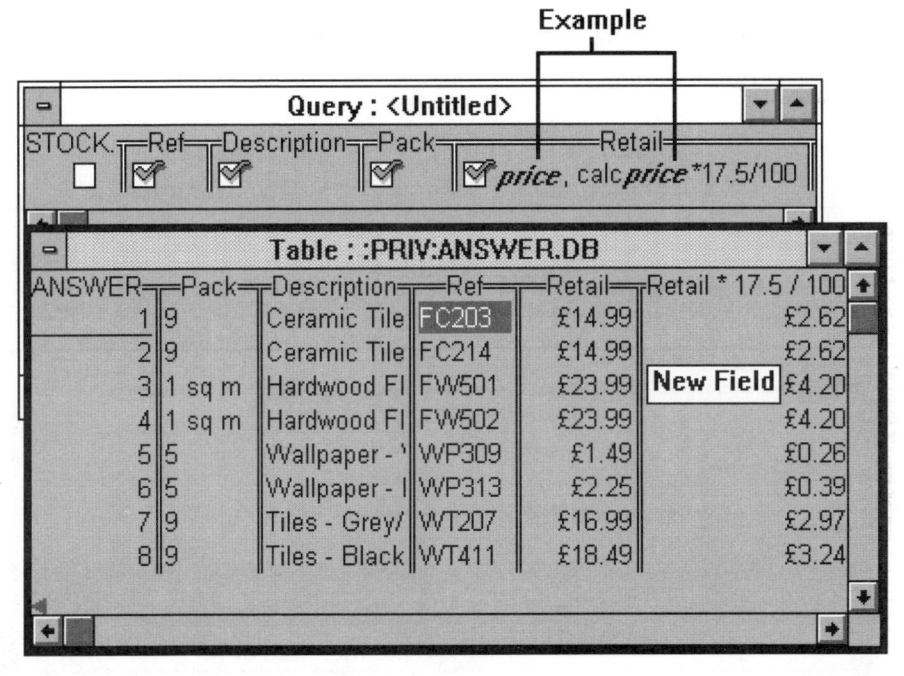

STOCK	Ref	Description	Pack	Retail
☐	☑	☑	☑	☑ *price*, calc *price**17.5/100

Query: <Untitled>

Table : :PRIV:ANSWER.DB

ANSWER	Pack	Description	Ref	Retail	Retail * 17.5 / 100
1	9	Ceramic Tile	FC203	£14.99	£2.62
2	9	Ceramic Tile	FC214	£14.99	£2.62
3	1 sq m	Hardwood Fl	FW501	£23.99	£4.20
4	1 sq m	Hardwood Fl	FW502	£23.99	£4.20
5	5	Wallpaper - '	WP309	£1.49	£0.26
6	5	Wallpaper - l	WP313	£2.25	£0.39
7	9	Tiles - Grey/	WT207	£16.99	£2.97
8	9	Tiles - Black	WT411	£18.49	£3.24

145

34 Calculations in Queries

If you wanted to find the cost of restocking items that were below reorder level, you could do it this way. (Assuming that you ordered the same number as the Reorder level.)

1. Start a new Query on the Stock table.

2. Find those below reorder level, as before. Create an example in the Reord field, and a '*<reord*' test in the Quantity field.

3. Create a second example in the Cost field. Write the calculation **CALC Cost * Quantity** in an unused field, or following one of the examples.

4. Run the query and compare your results with the screenshot. If you get something distinctly different, check the query carefully and run it again.

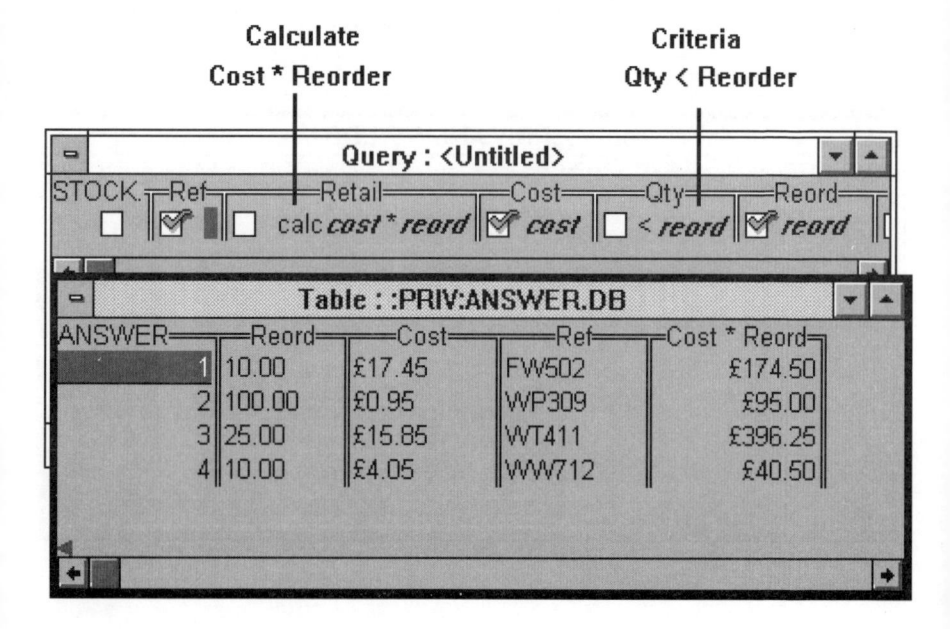

Calculate
Cost * Reorder

Criteria
Qty < Reorder

STOCK	Ref	Retail	Cost	Qty	Reord
□	☑	□ calc *cost * reord*	☑ *cost*	□ < *reord*	☑ *reord*

ANSWER	Reord	Cost	Ref	Cost * Reord
1	10.00	£17.45	FW502	£174.50
2	100.00	£0.95	WP309	£95.00
3	25.00	£15.85	WT411	£396.25
4	10.00	£4.05	WW712	£40.50

Renaming Answer Fields 35

You have seen how Paradox generates names for the new output fields based on the calculation. That last one, for instance, would have a new field titled 'Cost * Quantity'. This leaves you in no doubt about the contents, but you may want a different heading. That can be arranged.

The **AS** operator instructs Paradox to give a new name to the corresponding answer field. In that last example, if we wanted to call the calculated field 'Total Cost', the expression in the Query should read:

CALC Cost * Reord AS Total Cost

AS works with any field, not just those containing calculations. So, if you wanted the Cost field to be headed 'Purchase Price' in the answer table, you would write into the Cost field of the Query image the expression:

AS Purchase Price

We'll pull these ideas together to produce a valuation from our Stock file.

Stock Valuation

1. Open a New Query based on the Stock file. Mark the following fields for inclusion in the answer table: Ref No, Description, Pack, Type, Cost and Quantity.

2. Create the examples *Cost* in the Cost field and *Qty* in Quantity.

The calculation can go in any convenient field - I'm using Reorder Level. There's nothing else going in there, and it is easier to edit in

147

35 Renaming Answer Fields

an empty statement area. If you want the answer field to be renamed, then extend the expression to include **AS** ... You can see the calculation here - but with red where I have italics. Type them, in pressing [F5] before each of the examples.

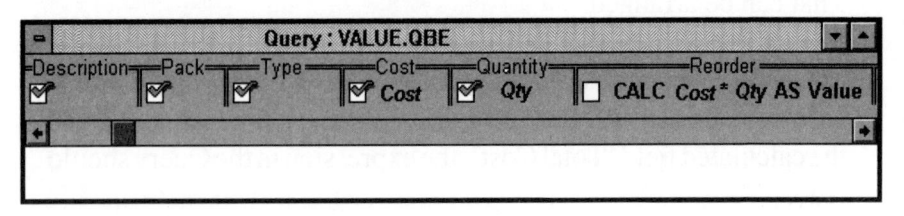

```
Query : VALUE.QBE
Description   Pack   Type      Cost      Quantity          Reorder
   ☑           ☑      ☑      ☑ Cost      ☑ Qty      ☐ CALC Cost * Qty AS Value
```

Run the query, and your answer table should look something like this. If you care to check the calculations, you'll find that the Value really does represent Cost x Quantity.

New Calculated Field

Ref No.	Description	Pack	Type	Cost	Quantity	Value
FC203	Ceramic Tiles - Marble 30x30	9	Floor	£9.23	120.00	£1,107.60
FC214	Ceramic Tiles - Grey 30x30	9	Floor	£8.79	60.00	£527.40
FW501	Hardwood Flooring - Ash	1 sq m	Floor	£17.45	20.00	£349.00
FW502	Hardwood Flooring - Beech	1 sq m	Floor	£17.45	8.00	£139.60
WP309	Wallpaper - Woodchip -11yd	5	Wall	£0.95	72.00	£68.40

Table : C:\PDOXWIN\ANSWER.DB

What we need now is the total value of all the lines of stock, and we can get that when we output the answer table as a report. But before we do that, there's another aspect of calculations that is worth a closer look.

Calculations in Reports 36

Our stock valuation query worked out the value of each stock line for us, but it didn't give us a total valuation for the whole stock. This is not something that we can find with a query - largely because the query's output is in terms of individual records, and there is nowhere it could place any kind of whole file summary. (There is a **SUM** operator for queries, but it is used for a completely different purpose.)

What can not be done with a query, can be managed with ease via a report, where there is a summary field facility. Try it with the stock valuation.

1. Run the valuation query and set up a new report based on the answer table. The default Tabular format will do fine, and there's no change to the Included Fields.

2. In the Report Design window, create a line space below the Value column. Click on the Field tool and set up a new field in the space. Open its Properties menu and set the display type to **Unlabeled** - the default label will be a meaningless field number and you can add explanatory text to beside it later.

3. Open the field's Properties menu again, and from the **Define Field** list, select ... from the top of the list. This takes you on to the **Define Field Object** dialog box. Creating the calculated field is easy enough as long as you do things in the right order - which is why there are numbers in the diagram.

149

36 Calculations in Reports

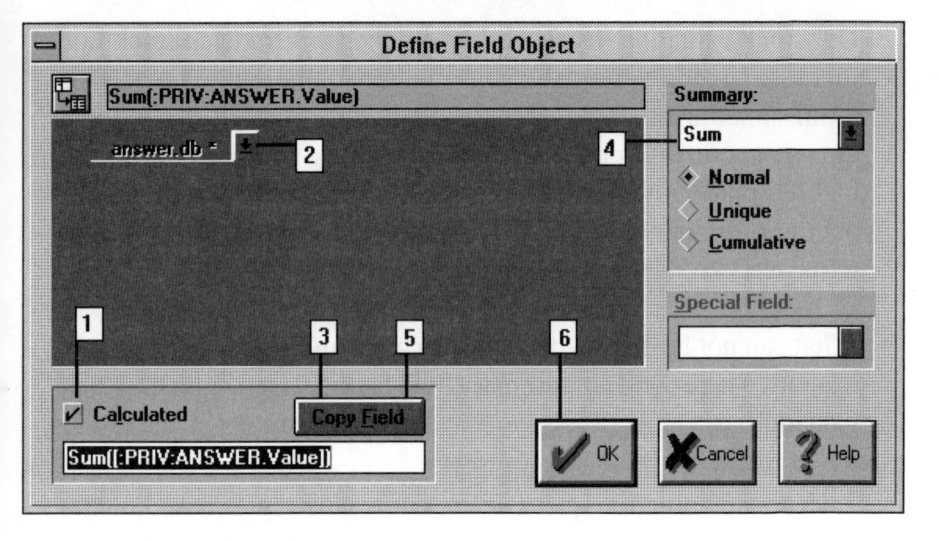

1. Select **Calculated**

2. Click the button beside the filename to pull down the field list and highlight the required field - here it will be 'Value'.

3. Click on the **Copy Field**. The name will be copied down into the slot at the bottom of the window.

4. Click on the **Summary** button and highlight **SUM**. (Or an alternative Summary function, as required.)

5. Click on **Copy field** again. The field definition will be rewritten to include the **SUM** function.

6. Click **OK** to exit back to the Report Design window.

When you preview the report, and you should find that the field contains the total of all the stock values. With my sample data, I get

150

Calculations in Reports   36

a total of £3,167.91 - low stock levels presumably being a reflection of the recession.

Ref No.	Description	Pack	Category	Cost	Quantity	Value
FC203	Ceramic Tiles - Marble 30x30	9	Floor	£9.23	120.00	£1,107.60
FC214	Ceramic Tiles - Grey 30x30	9	Floor	£8.79	60.00	£527.40
FW501	Hardwood Flooring - Ash	1 sq m	Floor	£17.45	20.00	£349.00
FW502	Hardwood Flooring - Beech	1 sq m	Floor	£17.45	8.00	£139.60
WP309	Wallpaper - Woodchip -11yd	5	Wall	£0.95	72.00	£68.40
WP313	Wallpaper - Embossed - 18yd	5	Wall	£1.45	40.00	£58.00
WT207	Tiles - Grey/Floral 11x11cm	9	Wall	£13.26	40.00	£530.40
WT411	Tiles - Black Diamond 20x20 cm	9	Wall	£15.85	15.00	£237.75
WW709	Cladding, T & G - 1800x10 cm	6	Wall	£4.89	24.00	£117.36
WW712	Shiplap Cladding - 1800x10cm	6	Wall	£4.05	8.00	£32.40

Total Stock Value £3,167.91

Other Formulae

Apart from **SUM**, Paradox offers these formulae:

- **Count** - gives the number of items in the set. Use this on the Reference Number or another required field, so that records are not missed out for lack of data in the counted field.

- **Min** and **Max** return the lowest and highest values.

- **Avg** is a simple arithmetic average - the sum of values divided by the number of them.

- **Std** is the Standard Deviation.

151

37 Catalogues from Files

This section is intended as a review of the sometimes tricky operations that we have covered in the last few sections. The aim is to produce a catalogue from the stock file. The catalogue will group the items by category, and display for each its reference, description, retail price and VAT. We'll also show a count of the number of items in each section and total items in stock. To do all this, we'll need a query that will filter out the required fields and calculate the VAT, and a report that has a group band and a calculated field.

The Query

1. Open a new query, selecting the Stock table.

2. Set the check marks to include the Ref Description, Pack, Type and Retail fields.

3. Move to the Retail field, press [F5] and write '*Price*' to create an example there.

4. Move to either the Reorder or Cost fields and type in this formula to calculate the VAT. Note that '*Price*' is an example, and that we are renaming the new field as VAT:

    CALC Price * 17.5/100 AS VAT

Save the query as 'Catalog' if you want to reuse it in a future session. If you like, use the Answer Table Properties menu to rename the table. This really doesn't matter, as you don't need to save the table. It can always be recreated from the query.

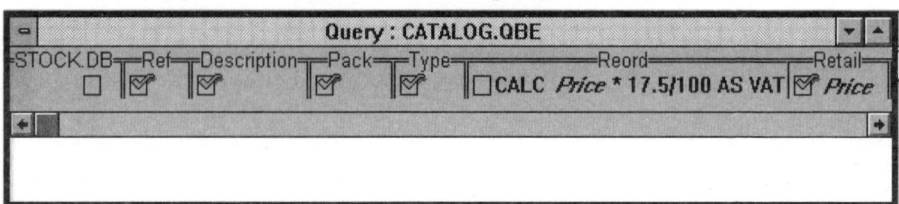

Catalogues from Files 37

Run the query and check the Answer table. It should be something like this. Everything OK? Now for the report.

answer	Ref	Description	Pack	Type	Retail	VAT
1	FC203	Ceramic Tiles - Marble 30x30	9	Paint	£14.99	£2.62
2	FC214	Ceramic Tiles - Grey 30x30	9	Floor	£14.99	£2.62
3	FW501	Hardwood Flooring - Ash	1 sq m	Floor	£23.99	£4.20
4	FW502	Hardwood Flooring - Beech	1 sq m	Floor	£23.99	£4.20
5	WP309	Wallpaper - Woodchip - 11 yd	5	Floor	£1.49	£0.26
6	WP313	Wallpaper - Embossed - 18yd	5	Wall	£2.25	£0.39
7	WT207	Tiles - Grey/Floral 11x11cm	9	Wall	£16.99	£2.97
8	WT411	Tiles - Black Diamond 20x20cm	9	Wall	£18.49	£3.24
9	WW709	Cladding, T & G - 1800x10cm	6	Wall	£6.99	£1.22
10	WW712	Shiplap Cladding - 1800x10cm	6	Wall	£5.99	£1.05

The Report

1. Open a new report, based on the Answer table.

2. At the Design Layout stage, select Single Record, Unlabeled and with the **By Row** layout - you want the fields to be placed across the screen.

3. Click on **Selected Fields** and remove Type. This isn't wanted in the main body of the report.

4. In the Report Design window, use **Add Band** to group the records on Type. The Type field will be added into the band heading. You may like to make this an Unlabeled field.

5. Up in the top Page band, highlight the <Today> object and press [Delete] to remove it. The date is scarcely necessary here. Likewise remove the file name.

153

37 Catalogues from Files

6. Add text for a page headers, them move down to the top group band and write the column headings in here. Click on the Text tool icon before each word so that they are separate. This will make it much easier to adjust them later. If they are written as a single line of text, the spacing between them will be changed if you change the font, and editing spaces is often awkward.

7. To get the number of items in each group, create a new field in the lower group band. Go through the **Define Field|...** sequence to get to the dialog box. Click on **Calculated**, then select Type from the Field list and Copy that it. Finally, select Count from the Summary options and Copy that into the definition.

8. Repeat the **Define Field** process in bottommost band, so that the Count of all stock items is displayed at the very end of the report.

The rest is up to you. Add decorative text, lines and boxes, etc, and set the field properties to get the Alignment, Fonts and Colors that you would like.

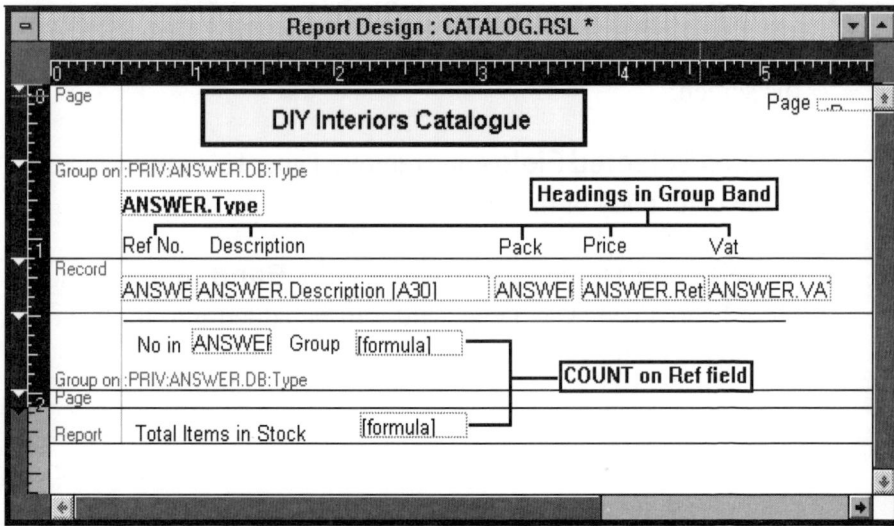

```
Report Design : CATALOG.RSL *

Page                                                              Page
              DIY Interiors Catalogue

Group on :PRIV:ANSWER.DB:Type
         ANSWER.Type                    Headings in Group Band
         Ref No.   Description          Pack    Price    Vat
Record
         ANSWE ANSWER.Description [A30]    ANSWEF ANSWER.Ret ANSWER.VA

              No in ANSWEF Group [formula]
Group on :PRIV:ANSWER.DB:Type                ─── COUNT on Ref field
Page
Report   Total Items in Stock  [formula]
```

154

Catalogues from Files   37

When you are reasonably happy with the design, preview the report to check the layout and that the formulae are working as they should.

DIY Interiors Catalogue

Page 1

Floor

Ref No.	Description	Pack	Price	Vat
FC203	Ceramic Tiles - Marble 30x30	9	£14.99	£2.62
FC214	Ceramic Tiles - Grey 30x30	9	£14.99	£2.62
FW501	Hardwood Flooring - Ash	1 sq m	£23.99	£4.20
FW502	Hardwood Flooring - Beech	1 sq m	£23.99	£4.20
WP309	Wallpaper - Woodchip - 11 yd	5	£1.49	£0.26

No in Floor   Group   5.00

Wall

Ref No.	Description	Pack	Price	Vat
WP313	Wallpaper - Embossed - 18yd	5	£2.25	£0.39
WT207	Tiles - Grey/Floral 11x11cm	9	£16.99	£2.97
WT411	Tiles - Black Diamond 20x20cm	9	£18.49	£3.24
WW709	Cladding, T & G - 1800x10cm	6	£6.99	£1.22
WW712	Shiplap Cladding - 1800x10cm	6	£5.99	£1.05

No in Wall   Group   5.00
Total Items in Stock   10.00

- 5 -
Graphical Displays

38 Graphic Objects

Graphic objects - scanned diagrams and photographs, images from a computer art package, captured screenshots or other picture files - can be imported into your Paradox reports, forms or tables. Paradox can cope with files in any of the standard formats - BMP, PCX, TIF, GIF and EPS. The image can be imported 'as is' or merged with graphics or text in a variety of ways. The picture can be left at its original size, shrunk or enlarged, or adjusted to fit a pre-defined boundary.

- The supplied sample Diveplan database shows how visually effective they can be. If you have not already done so, take ten minutes to have a tour through it and admire the tropical fishes! The screen refresh could be faster and smoother - though the jerkiness comes more from the way that Methods work, than from the presence of graphics. The screen display is smoother and faster when browsing directly through a file containing graphics.

Graphics in Reports

Putting pictures into reports - as the logo on the letterhead, perhaps - is a different matter. A small graphic will incur little cost in terms of speed or memory overheads, but can give an extra gloss to a printed report.

Importing a graphic is basically straightforward, though there are some potential traps. Tackle it this way, and you should avoid them.

If the image is to keep its original size:

1. Decide where the graphic is to go, and make some space for it.

Graphic Objects 38

2. Select the Graphic tool and drag an outline box. It doesn't matter if the outline is too small as the graphic will force it to the necessary size when it is imported.

3. Right click to get the **Properties** menu and select **Define Graphic|Paste From**.

4. At the **Paste From Graphic File** dialog box, select the image - resetting the Path if need be.

5. Click OK.

6. If you are in the top Page band, check that the bottom of the graphic is clear of the lower boundary. For some reason best known to itself, the first released version of Paradox cannot cope with graphics that touch this boundary.

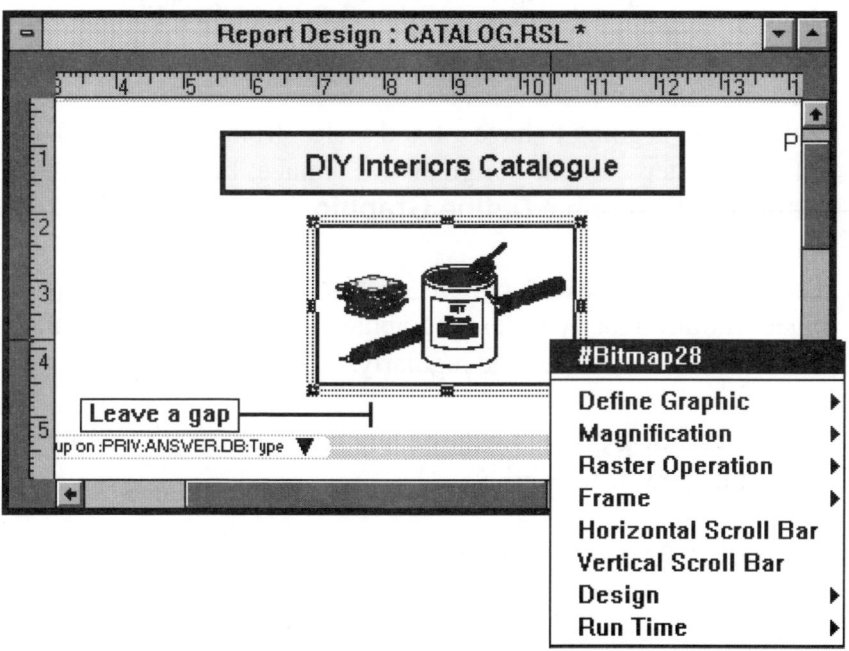

159

38 Graphic Objects

If the graphic must fit into a distinct space:

1. Check that you have enough room and adjust the bands if necessary.

2. Select the Graphics tool and draw an outline of the required shape. Check that this is clear of the lower boundary if the image is in the top Page band.

3. Right click in the outline to get the Properties menu and select **Magnification|Best Fit.**

4. Get the Properties menu again and work through steps 3, 4 and 5 as above.

The bands expand automatically to take large images, but do not shrink back again if the image is reduced. So, with Best Fit images, it saves work if you get the size right at the start.

If the image is going to have a fixed scale - from 25% to 400% - follow the steps for the 'original size' image, but selecting the **Magnification** before **Define Graphic.**

The **Raster Operation** options control how the image is combined with any underlying text or graphics. In practice there are only two that are likely to be used regularly:

■ **Source Copy** brings in the picture 'as is', obscuring anything that it happens to overlay.

■ **Source And** merges the image with any underlying detail using a Boolean AND. The technicalities of an AND operation on bitmapped images could take a couple of pages to explain, but the

160

Graphic Objects 38

basic effect is that background of the graphic becomes transparent, and some colours change when overlapped.

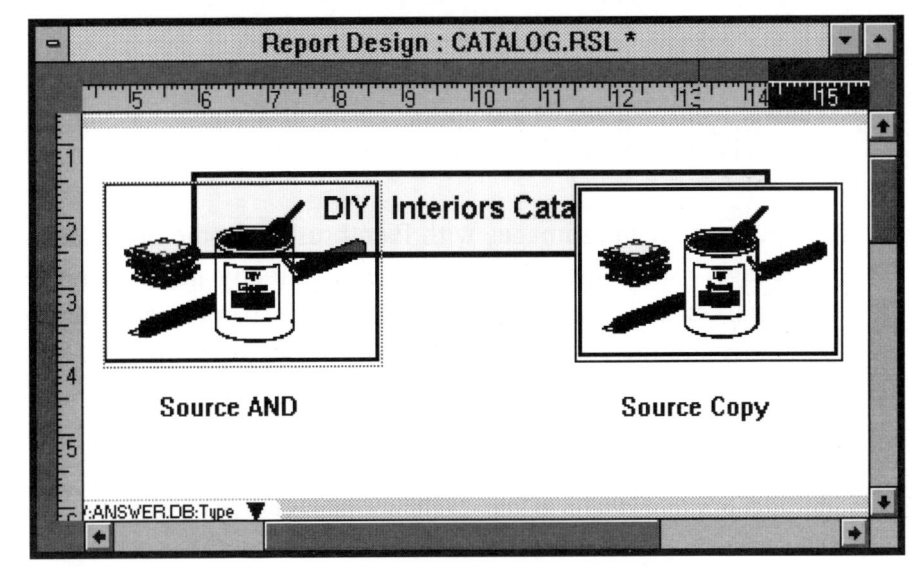

The other options may be useful in special situations. You can best see their effect by experimenting.

Graphics in Tables

If you do want to see how graphics work in tables, try it. You should have some suitable bitmap files in your system as there is a set supplied with Windows as alternative 'Wallpapers'. (And if you have deleted those files to save space on the hard disk, then you could to spend a few minutes with the Paintbrush package designing and saving some images of your own.

1. Set up a new table with a graphic field, or use **Table|Restructure** to add one to an existing table.

Graphic Objects

2. Take the table into Edit mode and click on the graphic field to highlight it.

3. Graphics from files can only be entered into the table through the **Edit** menu's **Paste From** option. Browse through the system to find the right directory and select a .BMP file.

4. If you are creating images with Paintbrush or some other art package, the image can be transferred directly through the normal Cut and Paste facilities. Cut it from the paint screen, and Paste it into the current graphic field with **Edit|Paste** or the **Paste** icon.

The table view normally allows too little depth in its lines to view a graphic properly. The form view is the sensible choice for graphics. Create a new form or add the new graphics field to an existing form.

Graphics in Forms

Where graphics are being used as decorations on a form, the techniques here are essentially the same as in reports. Where they are part of a database display, another factor comes into play. If you have an image which is larger than the space that you want to allocate to it, then rather than shrink it - and lose detail - you can add **Horizontal** and **Vertical Scroll Bars**. With these in place, image can be viewed at its original or enlarged size - albeit a section at a time.

OLE Objects 39

When you import a graphic, as a data item or a decoration for a report, the image is fixed even though the original file may later be changed or deleted. OLE objects are different. OLEs - Object Linked Embedded - retain their connection to the Server application program that created them. Try it and see.

1. Create an image in Paintbrush (or your favourite graphics package), and Copy it to the Clipboard.

2. Back in Paradox, open a form or report and use the OLE tool to create an outline box to take the object.

3. Get the object's **Properties** menu and select **Define OLE**. The one-option sub-menu **Paste PBrush** (or whatever application) will pop out. Click, and the OLE object is defined.

4. Run through that **Properties|Define OLE** sequence again, and this time you will have two choices. The **Paste ...** one would

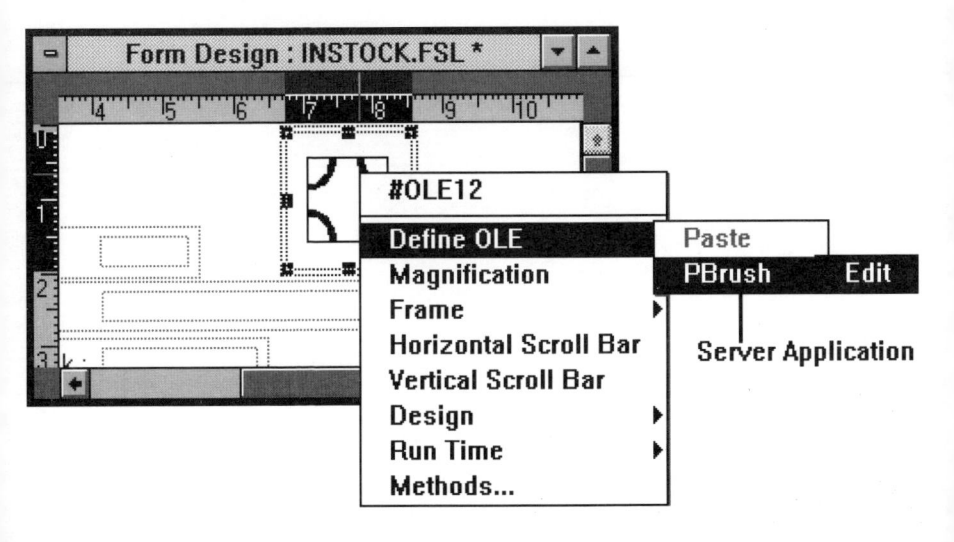

163

39 OLE Objects

replace the current graphic with whatever image happened to be in the Clipboard at the time to replace the current graphic. The second choice will have the name of the application. Click on that and again when you are offered **Edit**.

5. You will be taken out of Paradox to Paintbrush (or whatever application is the server for the graphic). Make your changes, and when you have finished, turn to its **File** menu. There will be two new options there. **Update** changes the image in Paradox. **Exit and Return to #OLE *xx*** takes you back to Paradox.

Graphic images are not the only kind of objects that can be embedded in a Paradox form or table using the OLE technique. Documents, tables and graphs from spreadsheets and part or whole documents from other applications can also be linked. But for that you need suitable applications, and the complexities inherent in this kind of linking takes us beyond the scope of this book

Crosstabs 40

Crosstabs offer a new way of looking at data. As the name implies, they cross-tabulate - draw together information from across the normal field and record structure. A typical use is to get total values, organised by one or more criteria, e.g. total income, broken down by payment method and sales person. As always, they best way to see what they are and what they do, is to work through an example.

We could create a crosstab from our existing tables, but there's little in any of them that will give a clear illustration. For this, we need a new table and suitable data. A simple petty cash database will do nicely. Each entry will record the date, amount, type of expenditure and the name of the spender. We can then use a crosstab to produce the total amount spent by each person, and the total spent by each person on each type of item.

You want a table that has data something like this:

PETTY2	Date	CostType	Amount	Spender
1	02/05/93	Travel	£15.52	John
2	02/05/93	Stationery	£2.35	Sally
3	03/05/93	Refreshments	£1.79	Sally
4	03/05/93	Travel	£5.68	Tim
5	04/05/93	Stationery	£14.99	John
6	06/05/93	Travel	£12.01	John
7	06/05/93	Refreshments	£2.34	Tim
8	09/05/93	Travel	£9.54	Sally
9	09/05/93	Refreshments	£7.95	John
10	10/05/93	Stationery	£0.86	Tim

You may like to add to the data, or use some of your own. The dates and amounts are unimportant, but do make sure that there are at least two entries with the same Spender and in the same Category.

165

40 Crosstabs

Use **File|New|Table** to set up a table with the field structure:

Field Name	Type	Size
Date	Date	
CostType	Alpha	12
Amount	Currency	
Spender	Alpha	12

Save it as 'petty', then type in the data.

Defining a Crosstab

A Crosstab is essentially a display object, and can only be created on a Form. As it will provide a summary of aspects of the whole file, it is probably best placed on a form by itself, rather than on one that also displays data from individual records. The form must be linked to a Data Model (table), if it is to have data to work on, but you don't want any fields. So, set it up this way.

1. Open a new form, but without selecting a data model, and get into Design mode.

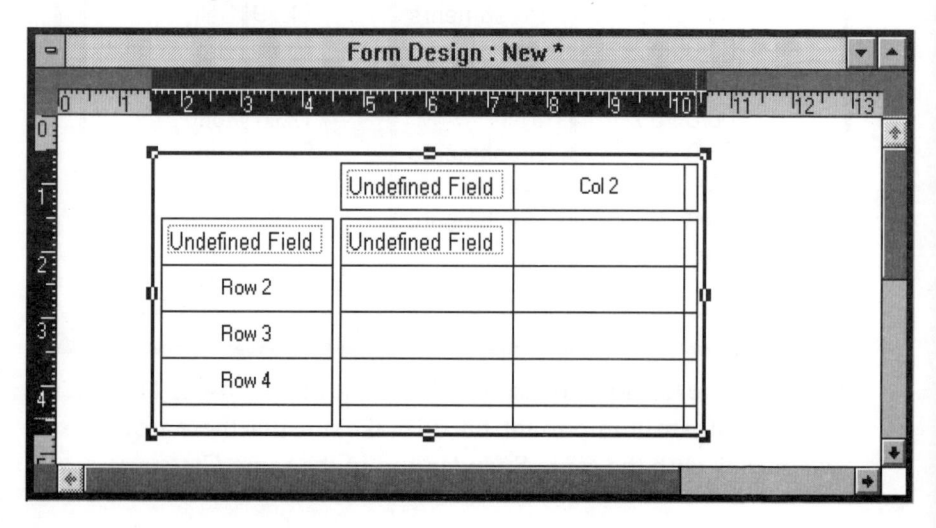

Crosstabs 40

2. Select the **Crosstab** tool. This is used like the Box tool. Drag the icon to make a rectangle that covers most of the width of the form, but relatively shallow. When you release the mouse button you will see a grid with row and column labels. The chances are that it will be the wrong size, chopping a column short and containing too many or not enough rows. Don't worry about it. It's easy to pull it to the right size later, when you have got some data in it.

3. Right-click somewhere within the grid - but not on a field - to get the properties menu and select **Define Crosstab**, then ... from its sub-menu. This will get you to the **Define Crosstab** dialog box.

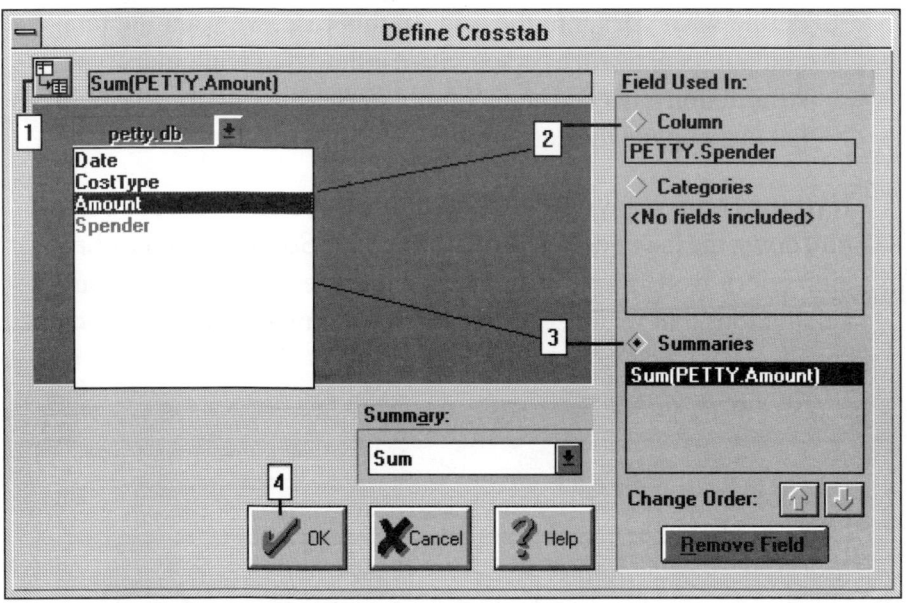

4. Click on the **Data Model** icon, in the top left corner. Select your 'petty' file from the list and click OK.

167

40 Crosstabs

Paradox now needs to know which fields are to be used. For the simplest type, you need only give it fields for the column headers and the grid contents.

5. Turn your attention to the right hand pane. You will see that under **Column** it says 'No fields included'. Go over to the left and click the arrow beside the table name to open the field list. Highlight the required field - in this case Spender. This will appear in the slot beneath **Column**. When the crosstab is viewed, there will be one column for each person who appears in this field - whether it is in only one record or in fifty.

6. Now click the radio button beside **Summaries**, and we will define what goes into the grid. In this case, we want the total amount spent by each person. **Sum** is the default Summary type, so no action is needed here. Simply select Amount from the field list to complete the definition.

If you had wanted any other type of summary, you would at this point pull down the list under the **Summary** (not *Summaries*) heading and select from there. You have the same range of summary calculations that you met earlier when creating Reports.

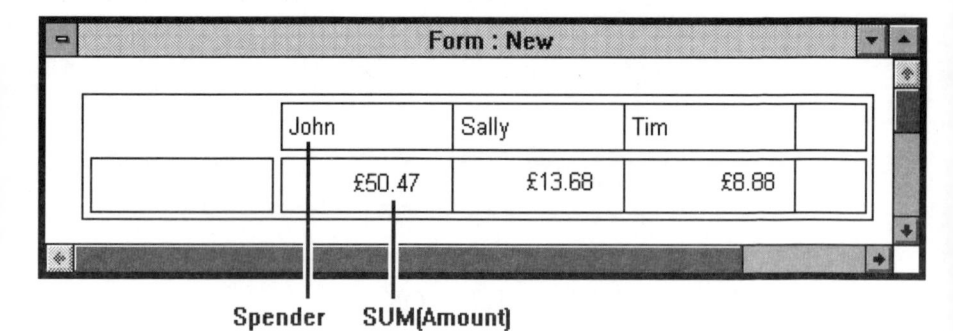

	John	Sally	Tim	
	£50.47	£13.68	£8.88	

Spender   SUM[Amount]

168

Crosstabs 40

7. Click OK to take you back to the Form, and once there, move to View mode. You should have something like the screenshot, showing each person's name and the total they have spent. If the grid isn't wide enough to include all the spenders, return to Design mode, highlight the crosstab and drag one or other side to expand it.

41 Two-Field Crosstabs

We can adapt this simple crosstab to bring in another field - CostType - to make it more truly 'cross-tabular'. It will then show the total Amount spent by each Spender under each CostType category.

In Design mode, highlight the crosstab and - if necessary - extend it downwards to give space for at least three rows. Pull down the crosstab's Properties menu and select **Define Crosstab|...** again.

Turn to the **Categories** slot. This handles the row headers. Click its button, then open the field list and select 'CostType'. Everything else remains the same.

Click OK, and View the redefined crosstab. If you compare the result with your original data, you should find that each cell contains a person's total spending under one cost category. Get your calculator out and cross check them with the figures in the table.

	John	Sally	Tim
Refreshments	£7.95	£1.79	£2.34
Stationery	£14.99	£2.35	£0.86
Travel	£27.53	£9.54	£5.68

Form : PETTY.FSL

Graphs

Graphs can be added to either Forms or Reports, and like Crosstabs, they provide an alternative - and sometimes more accessible - way of viewing data. They say 'a picture is worth a thousand words,' and it's probably just as true of graphs. Where a mass of numbers can confuse an issue, a graph can give a clear image of relationships and patterns of change.

Quick Graph

The **Quick Graph** routine provides the simplest route to creating a simple bar chart. All it wants from you is the fields to use for the labels along the bottom of the graph, and the figures to make into bars. Try it. You will need a suitable set of figures, so open the PETTY table, if it is not already on the Desktop.

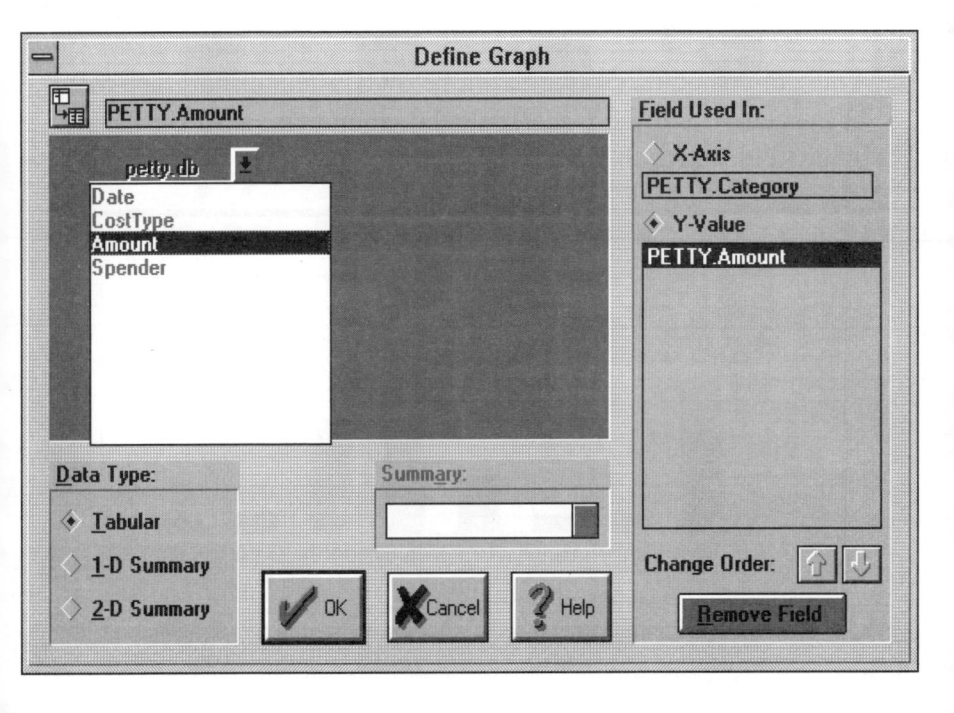

42 Graphs

1. Click on the **Quick Graph** icon or select the menu sequence **Table|Quick Graph**. The **Define Graph** dialog box will open.

2. It's waiting for you to tell it what field to use for the **X-Axis** - the labels across the bottom of the graph. Click on the arrow beside the table's name to open the field list and select either CostType or Spender.

3. Click the diamond beside the **Y-Value,** then go back and pull down the field list again.

4. You will see that only the numeric fields - and in this case that means just the Amount - are available to you. Select it, and click **OK** to finish.

Your graph should look like the one below. By default, the graph will be a bar chart, with the Y-scale calculated automatically from the Y-value field, and each Y-value charted separately.

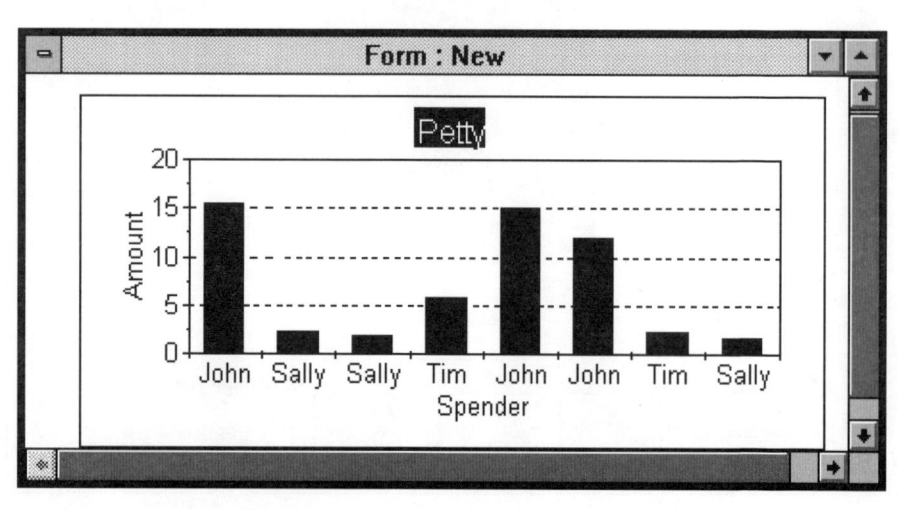

Graphs 42

The ways in which you can customise your graph displays are many and varied, and are controlled as usual by the Properties menus. To wrap up this section we'll take a quick dip into them.

1. Put the form back into Design mode. Place the mouse pointer within the graph frame, but outside the chart and away from the text labels. Click here and you'll get the main graph Properties menu. (Click elsewhere and you'll get the menus for the Title, X or Y Axes, the Y-values or the chart colours.)

2. Select **Data Type**. The default is **Tabular**, which graphs each value separately. Select **1-D Summary**. This will graph the total amounts under each X category. (The same choice can also be made when you start in the **Define Graph** dialog box.)

   You should see that you now have only three bars in your chart - though with empty slots to the right. We can eliminate these.

3. Open the main Properties menu again. This time, select **Min x-values** and set this to **3**.

4. Exit back to View mode, and your graph should be like this.

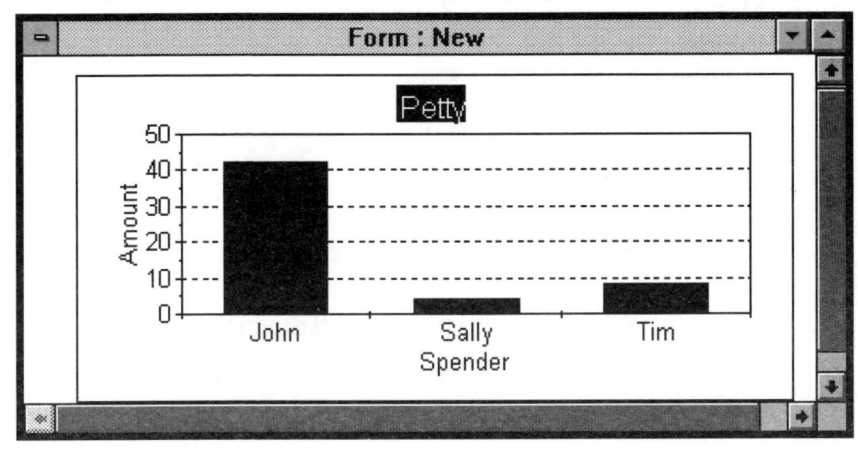

173

43 Multiple Series Graphs

A **Series** is a set of data that when plotted forms one line, or one set of bars, on a graph. In Paradox, when you assign a field to a Y-Value, it becomes a series.

You're going to need another new file if you want to see how multiple series graphs work, as none of the previous example tables have really suitable data. Something like this will do the job. This monthly summary of sales has three number fields, each of which can be plotted as a line, or set of bars, on a graph.

SALES	Month	Widgets	Gadgets	Gimbles
1	Oct	£15,000.00	£27,000.00	£12,000.00
2	Nov	£16,500.00	£25,000.00	£14,500.00
3	Dec	£15,750.00	£22,000.00	£16,000.00
4	Jan	£16,000.00	£21,000.00	£17,500.00
5	Feb	£15,000.00	£19,000.00	£19,000.00
6	Mar	£14,500.00	£17,500.00	£21,250.00

1. Create the table, using the definition:

Field	Type	Size
Month	Alpha	3
Widgets	$	
Gadgets	$	
Gimbles	$	

2. Type in the data then click on Quick Graph.

3. In the **Define Graph** dialog box, select Month as the X-Axis.

4. Click on the **Y-Value** radio button, pull down the field list and highlight each of the other three fields. All will be copied into the Y-Value list.

174

Multiple Series Graphs 43

5. Select **1-D Summary**, and exit with OK. The initial graph should look like this.

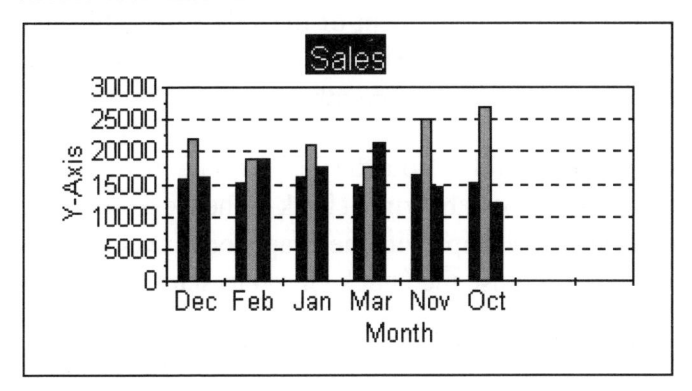

6. If you want to know what the bars mean - always a good idea when you have more than one series - go into Design mode, get the Properties menu and select **Options|Show Legend**.

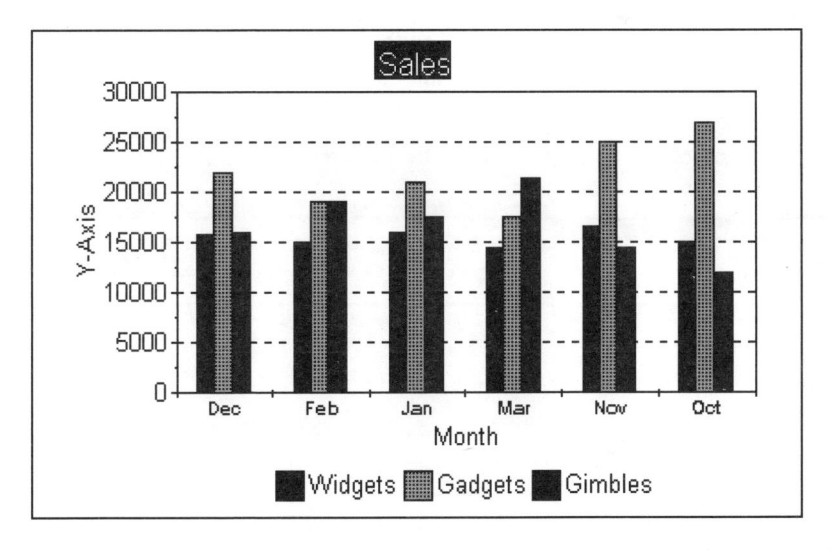

A bar chart is not necessarily the best way to view this data, as you will see when we look at some of the alternatives in the next section.

43 Multiple Series Graphs

2-D Summary Graphs

These are the graphed equivalent of the 2-D Crosstabs, and are created in much the same way. They will display your monthly sales by region - or regional sales by month.

They can be best illustrated from the PETTY data. If you saved the from with the 2-D Crosstab, bring it back to the Desktop in Design mode and set up a new graph with the Graph tool. If you didn't save it, open the table and use the Quick Graph to start the process.

1. In the Define Graph dialog box select **2-D Summary** in the **Data Type** box. A new area, headed **Grouped By** appears in the right hand pane.

2. Select Spender as the X-Axis, CostType as the Grouped By field and Amount as the Y-Value. Click OK to exit.

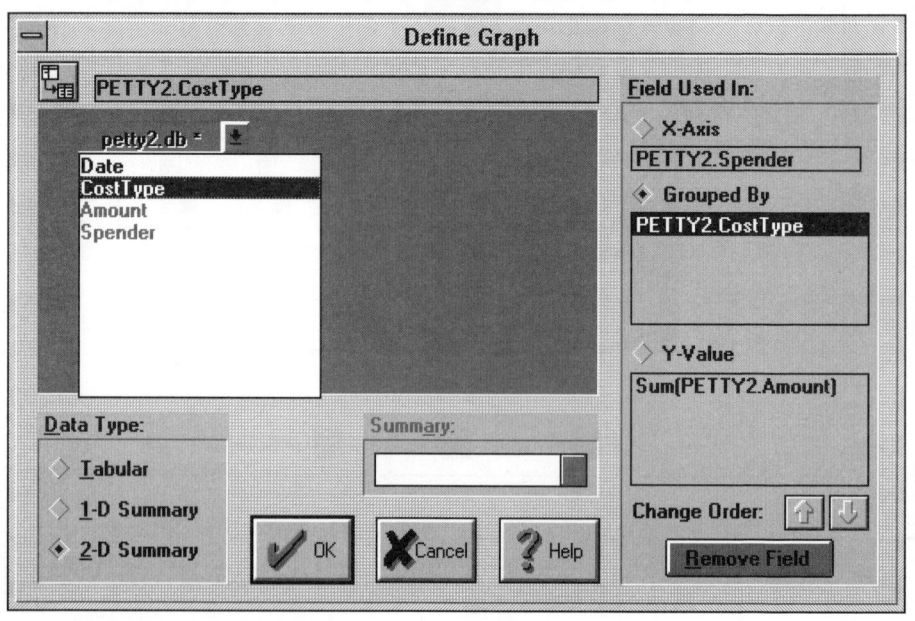

176

Multiple Series Graphs 43

3. Turn on the **Options|Show Legend** so that you know what the graph is all about, and have a look at it. You may notice that the 'Grouped By' field has been incorporated into the heading - all part of Paradox's user-friendly service.

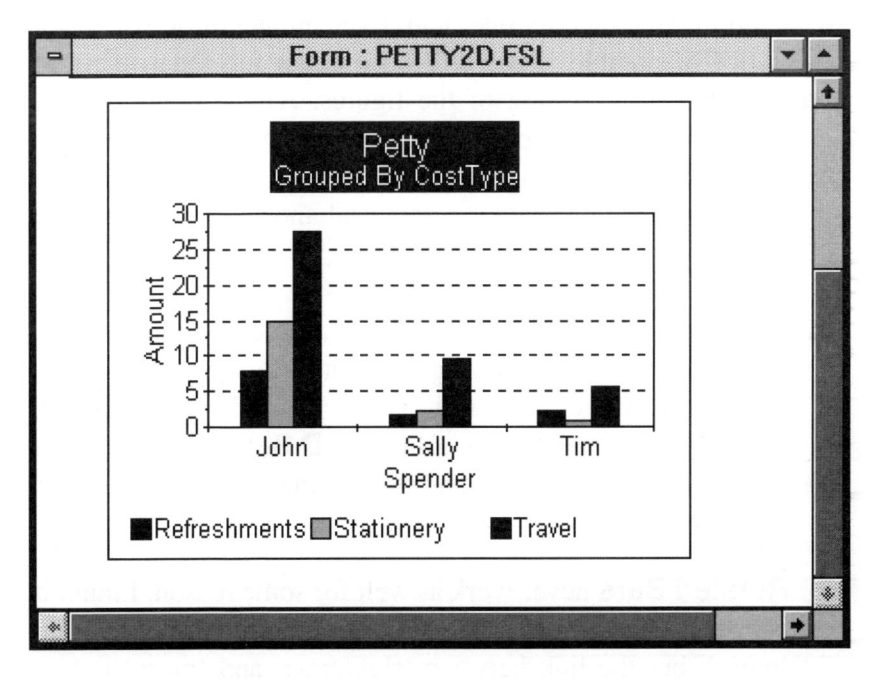

44 Alternative Graph Types

Single Series Graphs

The **Graph Type** menu offers 16 different ways of displaying your data. Not all of these are suitable for use with single series graphs - i.e. those based on only one field. Even among those which are theoretically suitable, some will do a better job than others of bringing out the meaning of the figures. A well-chosen graph highlights relationships between values and makes comparisons easier; a badly chosen graph obscures those relationships. Finding the right type for your data is partly trial and error, but there are certain guidelines.

- **Bar** charts allow simple comparisons between separate items. They work well here, showing clearly how John spends far more petty cash than either Sally or Tim. The plain **2-D Bar** is probably clearest in this case. In the **3-D Bar**, the names along the X-axis tend to overlap and must be taken down a couple of font sizes.

- **Rotated Bars** never work as well for some reason. I think it is because there is a simple connection between 'higher' and 'more', but the link between 'rightmost' and 'more' is less immediate. The **3-D Step** is variety of bar chart, but with no spaces between the bars.

- **Line** graphs are good for showing trends over time, for there is an implied continuity of change between the marked points. For this same reason they make comparison between separate items less clear.

- **Pie** charts show how components relate to the whole. In this case they show that John doesn't just spend more than either Sally or Tim, he spends a lot more than both of them together.

Alternative Graph Types   44

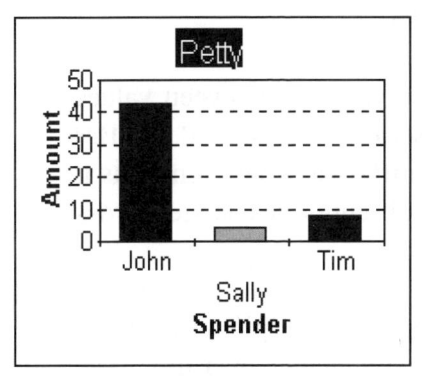

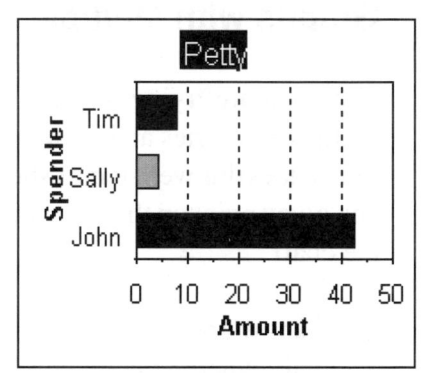

2-D Bar

2-D Rotated Bar

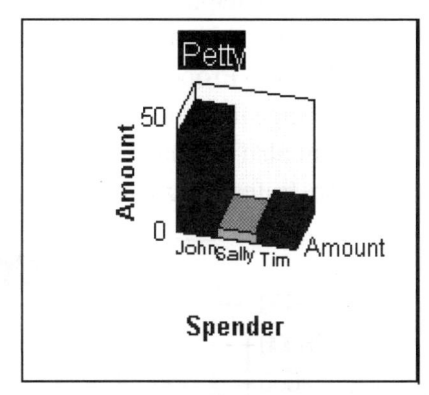

3-D Bar

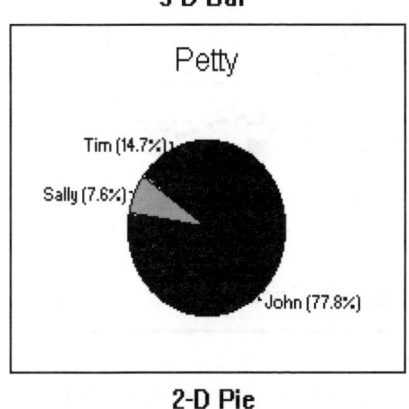

3-D Step

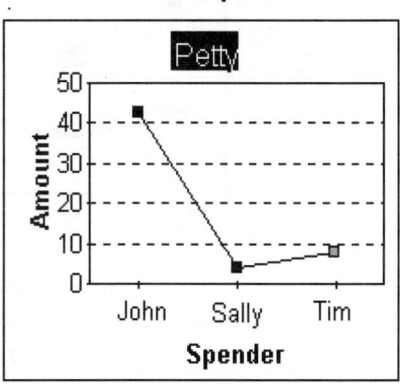

2-D Pie

Line

44　Alternative Graph Types

Graphs with Multiple Series

Here you are trying to bring out the variation between values within each series and between the series. The standard 2-D Bar rarely does this well. It may show the differences between items at any given point on the X-Axis, but it obscures the changes across the chart.

- A **Line** graph is often the answer with multiple series, especially where you are concerned with change over time. The default display uses thin lines with coloured squares to mark the points. This can be readily improved upon. Right click on a line to get its Properties menu and look at the Line options. You can change the colour, thickness and style of the lines; the Marker can also be changed. The overdone display shown here demonstrates what can be done if you get carried away.

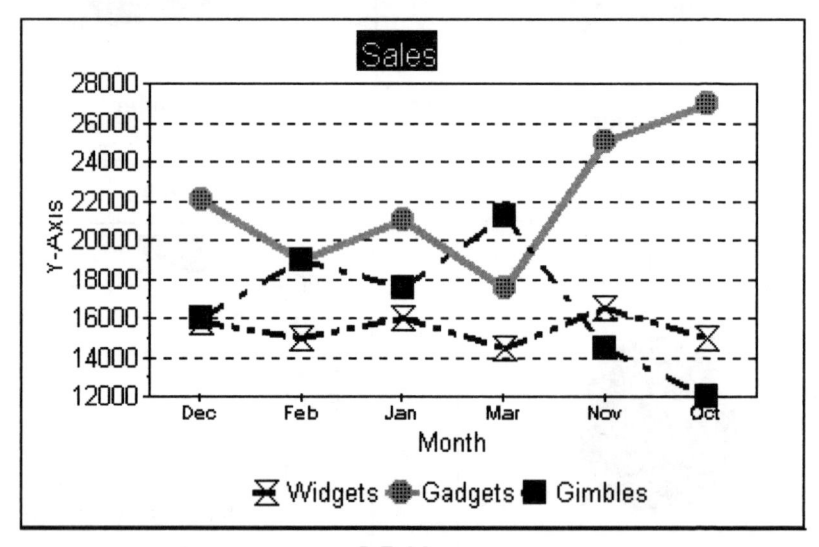

2-D Line

Alternative Graph Types 44

- A **3-D Bar** will sometimes work with multiple series, but only if the rearmost values are generally higher than those in the front. This is not the case with the sample data we have here!

- **3-D Ribbon** is essentially the same as the Line graph, but with added width. It suffers from the same problem as the 3-D Bar - the series at the back can be obscured by those in front.

With any of the 3-D types, you may find that the display can be improved by adjusting the **Rotation** and **Elevation** - both on the **Properties|Options** menu. These change the viewing angle and by turning one way or the other, you can sometimes make the back series more visible.

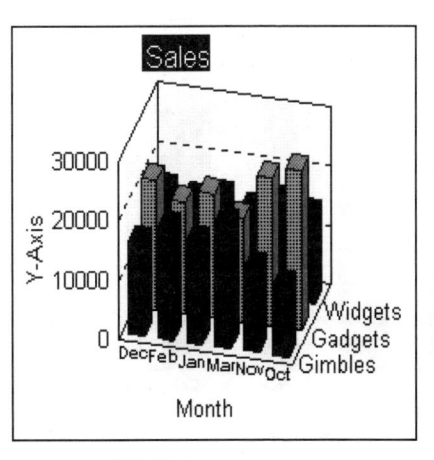

3-D Bar

Ribbon

- **Area** graphs and **Stacked Bars** are both good for showing cumulative totals, though with some loss of clarity as regards individual series. In the examples here, you can see that overall sales stay much the same throughout the period, and it is also clear that the Widget sales - the bottom value - are fairly stable.

181

44   Alternative Graph Types

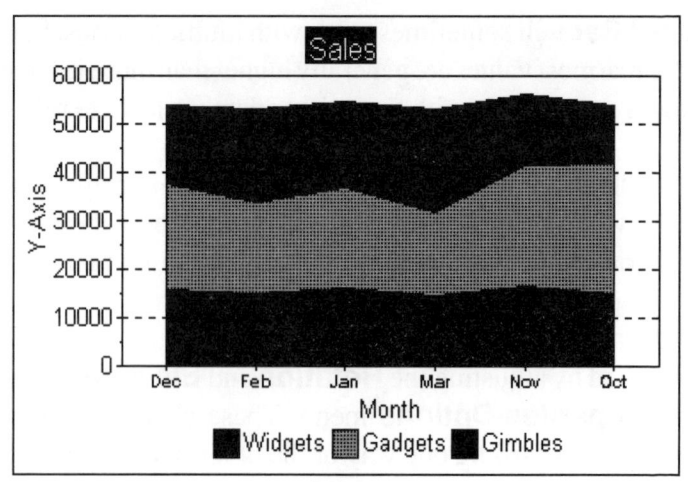

Area

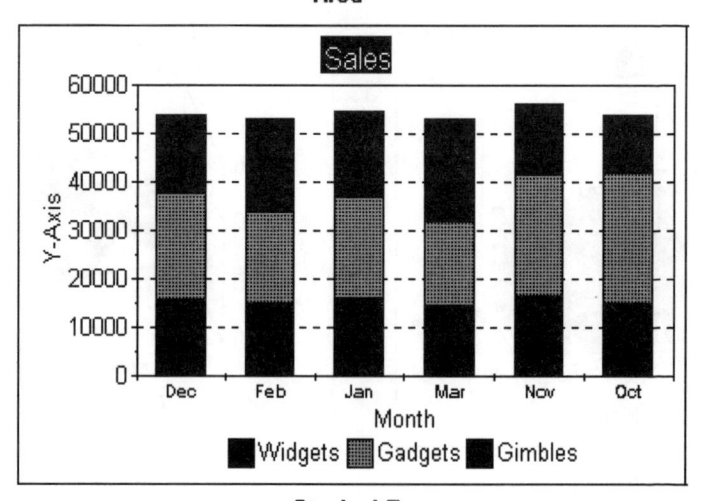

Stacked Bar

The rise in Gadget sales is less clear, and the fall in Gimble sales is nothing like as noticeable here as it is in a Line graph. Sometimes it is useful to be able to play down the failures.

Alternative Graph Types 44

- The **Columns** display is a variation on the **Pie** chart. Each column contains the value from one series, but with each value coloured differently and the percentage contribution of each to the whole shown by the side. It really doesn't work with this sample data for several reasons. It is best where there are significant differences between the values in each series, and where there are fewer values - not the case here.

Bar, Area, Stacked Bar, Columns and Pie are also available in 3-D versions. I find the added depth a bit of a gimmick and prefer the clarity of the 2-D images.

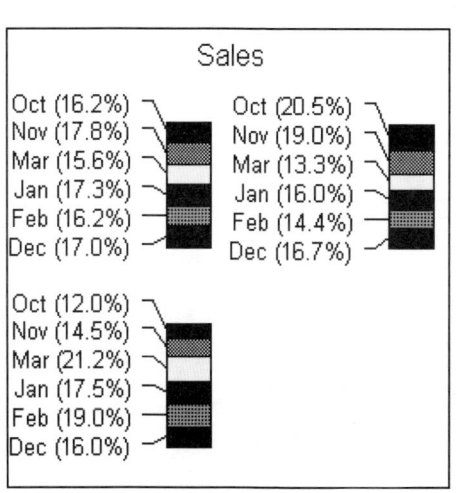

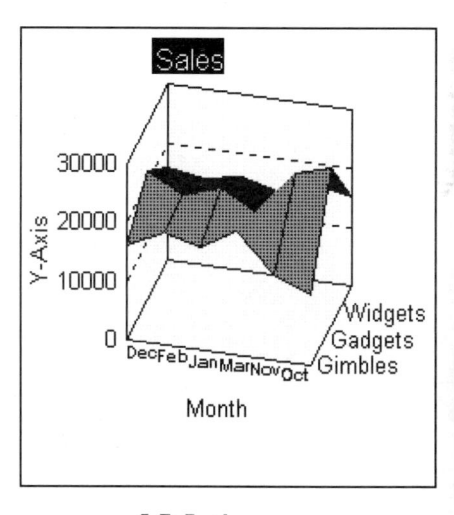

2-D Columns

Sales

Oct (16.2%)
Nov (17.8%)
Mar (15.6%)
Jan (17.3%)
Feb (16.2%)
Dec (17.0%)

Oct (20.5%)
Nov (19.0%)
Mar (13.3%)
Jan (16.0%)
Feb (14.4%)
Dec (16.7%)

Oct (12.0%)
Nov (14.5%)
Mar (21.2%)
Jan (17.5%)
Feb (19.0%)
Dec (16.0%)

3-D Surface

- The **3-D Surface** graph produces an intriguing image, though not one that is particularly suitable for the sample data. It is very good at picking out highs and lows from a mass of figures, and for showing change in two dimensions. I suspect it is of most use for scientific analysis. You could even use it to create relief maps, plotting heights at different latitudes and longitudes - but I wouldn't fancy typing in all the necessary figures!

183

- 6 -
Methods

45 Automated Systems

The Paradox package includes ObjectPAL, the Programmable Application Language. I suspect that those readers who are not programmers may well be saying, "This is where I get off." Don't. Bear with me a little longer, for you don't need to be an expert programmer to make effective use of ObjectPAL.

It can be used to create complete applications programs - i.e. fully automated systems with their own menus and commands that run independently of the main Paradox structure. To write ObjectPAL programs to that level, you would either need prior experience in programming or be prepared to take time to acquire the expertise. But you don't need to write at that level to put ObjectPAL to good effect.

Once you start to use Paradox for real applications, you will find that there are some sequences of operations that you perform regularly and always in the same way. With a stock control system, for instance, you might well want a weekly re-order list. (The query and report layout for this would have been done once and saved as files.) Working from the Desktop, you would open the reorder query, run it, open the report file and send it for printing. It shouldn't take long - no more than a dozen or so keystrokes or mouse moves and clicks - but it would be more convenient to reduce this to a single operation. Quite apart from making it quicker for you, it would also make the job easy enough to be done by another person, who knows less about Paradox and your stock system.

Writing a set of ObjectPAL methods to do this kind of job does not require any great expertise. A few hours' work will give you all you need to work at this limited - but useful - level. Work through the next few sections and you will see.

Automated Systems 45

You will soon realise that with a little more time spent on exploring the possibilities of ObjectPAL, and a bit more effort in planning, you can create significantly more complete applications. You may even catch the programming bug!

46 Scripts and Methods

With ObjectPAL you are into **OOPS** - **O**bject-**O**riented **P**rogramming. Translated into English that means that it revolves around objects - buttons, menus, forms and the rest. The basic definitions for these exist already, and the system knows, in outline, what to do with one when it meets one. Your role is to specify the properties of the object and the nature of the actions that are linked to it. And that's not as bad as it sounds because the actions will all relate to objects - and the system knows how to handle them.

It is 'event-driven' language in that the program code is executed in response to an event. This may be the opening of a form, a click on a button, a mouse moving over a field or whatever. The event may be performed by the user or by another piece of code.

The code can be written in two forms - as a **script** or a **method**.

- A script is similar to a 'normal' computer program, in that it is a text file containing a sequence of instructions, and it exists as a separate object in its own right. You will see 'Script' in the list of file types in the speedbar and when you run a **File|Open** or **File|New** command.

- A method is a piece of code attached to an object that defines how that object will respond to an event. In general, methods have more limited and clearly defined functions, and are easier to write. The fact that any given method does very little is by no means restrictive. A single object may have several methods attached to it. With as form, for example, there may be one method to control what happens when the form is opened, another for when it closes, a third to handle a menu that has been written into the form. A form may also have other objects on it - buttons, fields, boxes and graphics. Each of these may have a set of methods attached to them.

Scripts and Methods 46

Complex and sophisticated applications can be created by separate, but linked, methods within a form. It is similar to the approach taken with mainstream computer languages, where programs are built up from largely self-contained procedures. There are three clear advantages to this approach.

■ Each individual method (or procedure) can be tested separately - and as they tend to be short and to the point, errors are much easier to indentify.

■ The structure can be easily adapted or extended. You can start with a very simple application and over time add extra facilities, or enhance those already there.

■ You can copy methods from one application to another, where the same or similar operations are required. Once you have written a method to automate the printing of reports, the next time you need a report-printer, you can copy that method into your new application. All it will need is a couple of minutes' editing to change the filenames.

Let's see how this works out in practice.

47 Buttons

Buttons probably provide the simplest point of entry into Object-PAL. In this section we will set up a form containing a button which displays messages when pressed. Though thoroughly trivial, it demonstrates a number of key concepts about method-writing.

First we need a form on which to place the button. It can be blank - there's no point in linking it to any data table. Give the command sequence **File|New|Form**, and at the Data Model dialog box, press OK without selecting a table.

1. When you reach the Form Design screen, select the **Button** tool and place a button somewhere on the form. (Use the Button tool as you do the Box tool, by dragging an outline to the required shape.)

2. The new button will have the word 'LABEL' written on it. To change this to something more meaningful, position the cursor on the word and click twice to get the text cursor. Erase 'LABEL' and type 'Press Me' - or whatever label you want.

The button object will have been named as #button1 (or some other number) by the system. This can also be changed to something more meaningful. It is not essential in this simple one-object example, but when you start to write more complex systems a meaningful name will make it much easier to identify which button does what.

3. To rename it, highlight the button and right click to get the Properties menu. Select **Title Bar** to open the **Object Name** dialog box.

| Buttons 47 |

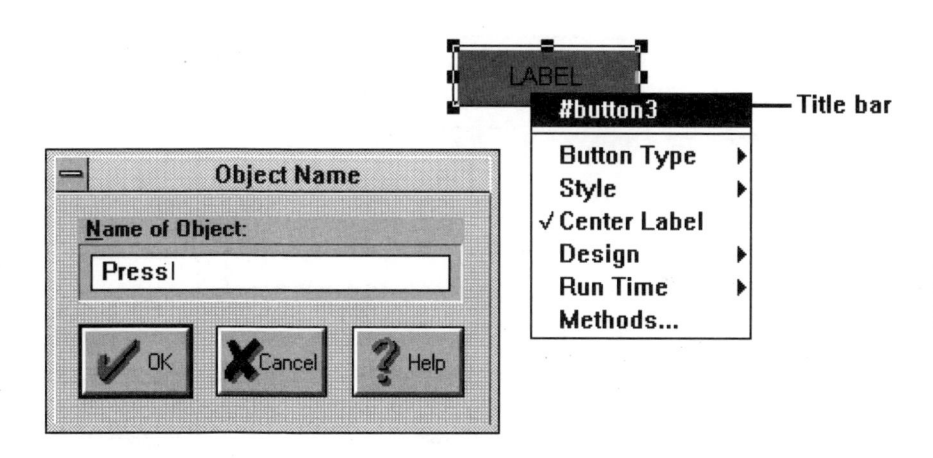

4. Type in the new name and press OK. This name must be a single word, but - unlike a filename - there is no limit on its length. ObjectPAL has a convention that where a name consists of two or more words, they are run together but with the first letter of each capitalised. So, if you wanted to call this the 'press me button', the name should be written 'PressMeButton'.

Now for the method. We are going to make the button display the message "Ouch, Not so hard" when it is pressed.. Most of this can be achieved using the **Built-in Methods**. These are not complete ready-written methods, but rather frameworks containing - invisibly - the code that handles events relating to the object. Their names are good indications of the events that they handle. First in the button methods list, for instance is 'pushButton' which handles a press on the button. Let's find it.

5. Right click the button to get the Properties menu again, and select **Methods**. The **Methods** dialog box will open.

191

| 47 | Buttons |

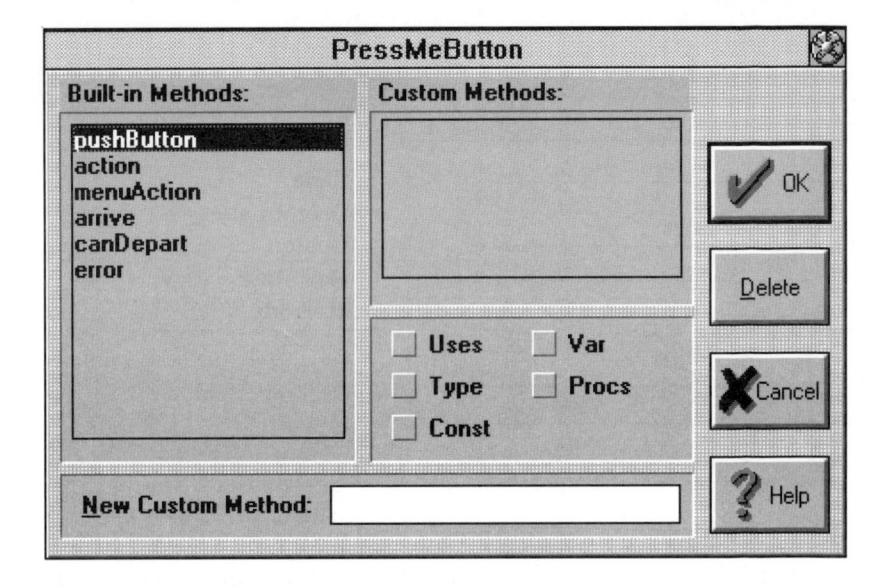

```
                    PressMeButton
Built-in Methods:    Custom Methods:
 pushButton
 action
 menuAction                                    ✓ OK
 arrive
 canDepart
 error                                         Delete

                     ☐ Uses    ☐ Var
                     ☐ Type    ☐ Procs         ✗ Cancel
                     ☐ Const

New Custom Method: [              ]            ? Help
```

6. At this stage we are only interested in the left hand pane, which contains a list of Built-in Methods. Highlight **pushButton** and click OK.

The method appears in a window, titled with the object's and the method's names. Initially it will consist only of the header and footer line. Apart from taking care not to change them, you don't need to bother much about these lines. The header identifies the method and the variables (temporary data stores) through which information is passed to and from the method. The footer marks its end. Your bit - the code that sets out the details of what the method will do - goes in the space between.

In this case we want a message to appear on the screen when the button is pressed. The message will be written in an information dialog box. The command word for this is **msgInfo** and you must supply a title for the box and the message. These are written in

Buttons   47

brackets after the command, with each string enclosed in quotes and a comma to separate them. All action commands are followed by brackets into which you put the specific data needed for the action.

7. Edit the method to give you something like this - use your own title and message if you prefer.

method pushButton(var eventInfo Event)
msgInfo("Ouch","Not so hard!")
endmethod

8. When you think you have got it right, check it. Pull down the new **Language** menu and select **Check Syntax**. This serves a double purpose. It scans through your text and reports any errors - its main purpose - but if everything is OK, it also saves the method at the same time.

Syntax Errors

Error reports tend to be rather cryptic. This is a bit inevitable, as the syntax checker can only go by what you have actually written, and not by what you intended. If you have spelt a key word wrongly, or missed out some punctuation or part of a command line, it won't necessarily know what you were trying to do. There is a further problem that once it has hit an error, it may not be able to make sense of what follows - if it can't see where one bit ends, how can it know where the next begins? So, note any error reports and try to get what you can from them.

A better guide to the problem is to look for the cursor. This should be positioned close to the error. Check the line containing the cursor before looking any further.

193

| 47 | Buttons |

9. Once the method passes the syntax check, close its window and switch the form into View mode so that you can test it. Click on the button and you should see your "Ouch" message.

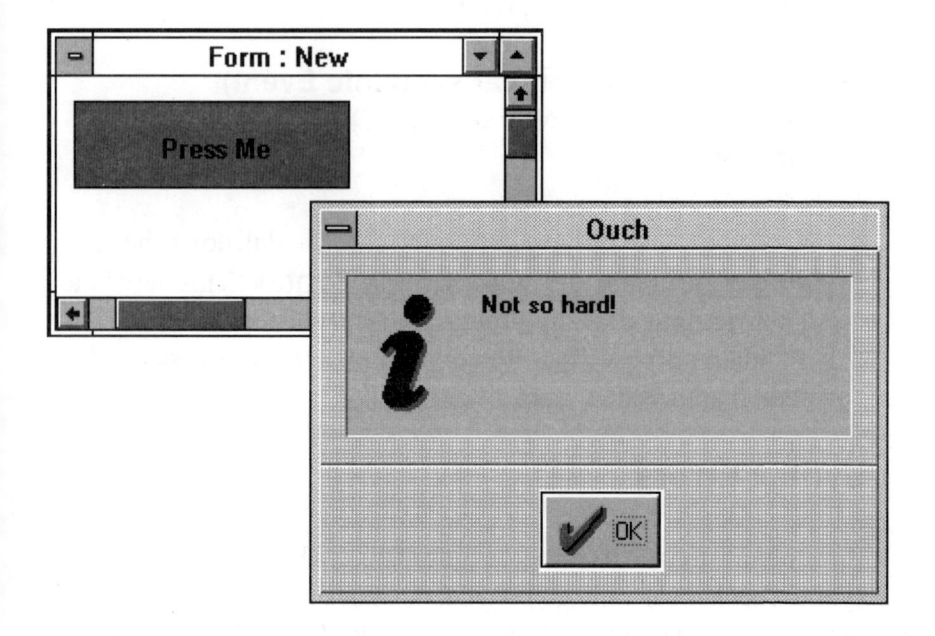

Conditional Actions   48

A method may have one active line - and still be useful nontheless - or it may contain a whole set of instructions. These may form a simple sequence, with each following directly after the previous, or the flow of execution may be dependent upon certain conditions. The method may offer the user a number of alternatives, or an option to stop an action. If it is designed to open a file, for instance, it should check that the file is there and take appropriate action if it is not.

The simplest way to make the flow branch, is to use the **if** command. To see how this works, we'll build on our button method, adding a **Yes/No/Cancel** dialog box and handling the user's response.

1. Put the form back into Design mode, get the button's Properties menu and select Methods. In the Methods dialog box you will see that pushButton now has an asterisk next to it. This shows that the method exists. Highlight it and press OK, to open its editing window.

2. Move the text cursor to the end of the **msgInfo** line and press [Enter] to open up a new line. Add new text so that your method looks like this:

   method pushButton(var eventInfo Event)
   msgInfo("Ouch","Not so hard!")
   if msgYesNoCancel("Button Use","Will you be gentle next time?") = "No"
      then msgInfo("Beast", "I shall sulk")
   endif
   endmethod

There are a couple of different things happening here. Let's take them one at a time.

195

48 Conditional Actions

msgYesNoCancel(*title,question*)

This sets up a dialog box with three buttons labelled, "Yes", "No" and "Cancel". You supply the title and the question. If you don't like mine in the examples, write your own. Both title and question must be enclosed in quotes, and they are separated by a comma. When the user clicks a response to the dialog box, the reply will be passed back to the method as either a "Yes", "No" or "Cancel" string. The method can pick this up and act on it.

if test is true
    then perform action(s)
endif

With **if ... then ... endif** we can control the flow within methods. When excution reaches this point, the system evaluates the expression that follows the '**if**'. If it is true - in this case if the msgYesNoCancel box has produced a "No" response - the action following '**then**' is performed. If it is false, the action is ignored. There may be any number of actions after '**then**', all of which are dependent upon the truth of the '**if**' test. The **endif** word marks the end of these conditional actions.

3. Check the syntax of the revised method, and if all is well, go to View mode and press the button. You should see the original message box followed by the **Yes/No/Cancel** box.

You might like to edit the method to produce a different message. If you want this be displayed on two or more lines, write the line breaks into the string by pressing [Enter]. No special punctuation is needed for multi-line strings. Here, for instance, the message is spread over three lines:

196

Conditional Actions 48

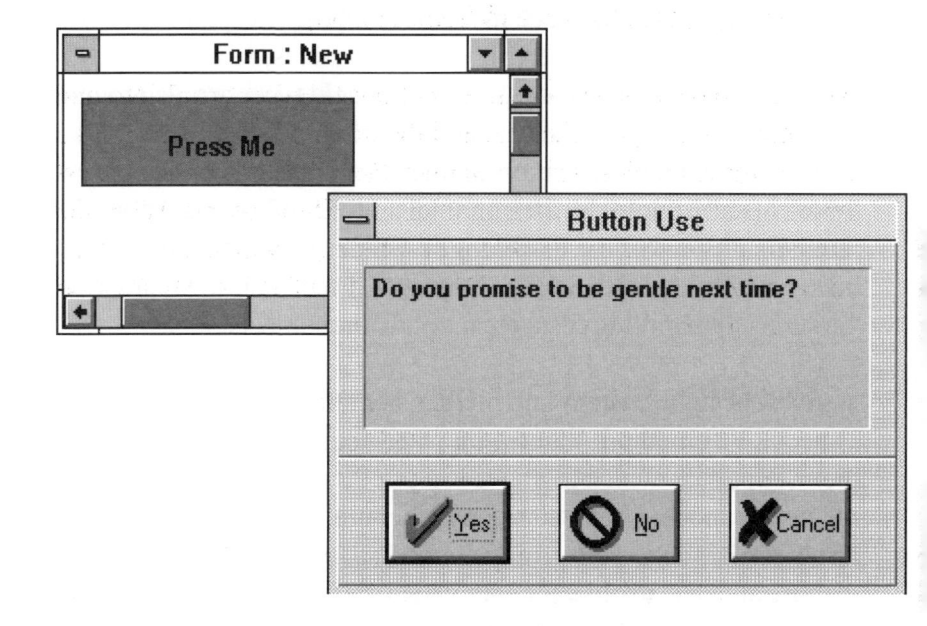

msgInfo("Problems?", "In case of difficulty, contact: John, Room 214
or Call Ext. 123")

if ... then ... else ...

With **if ... then ...** the structure is like a detour on a road. If the test proves true, the method flows round the detour. If not, it goes straight past. Either way, it gets to the same point. In this case, that was the end of the method, but there could have been further actions after the **endif**. Sometimes, you will want the method to branch like a T-junction, with the flow going either one way or the other. For this, we need another version of the structure - **if ... then ... else**. And for that we need variables.

49 Variables

A **variable** is a named place in memory where data can be stored. There are a number of different types of variables, each designed to hold a different type of data. Most of the field types are also found as variable data types - date, currency, logical, memo, number, graphic - but there are others specific to ObjectPAL. There are SmallInt and LongInt for storing small (+/- 32767) and large whole numbers. Instead of the fixed length Alphanumeric field type, you have a variable length String. As you will see later, there are also variables for handling files, menus and other objects.

Variables can be written into methods or attached to an object via a special **Var** method. Where you place your variables determines their scope - i.e. which methods can use them. A variable within a method cannot be accessed by any other method; if it is attached to an object, it is accessible to any method attached to the object - and to those attached to objects contained in the first object. In practice, what this means is that if the variables are written into a form, they are visible to all methods on the form, and to those on the buttons, tables and boxes that are on the form. But let's take it a stage at a time.

Creating a Variable

1. Go back to your form, in Design mode, and open up the Methods dialog box for the button. The lower right pane holds a set of cryptically labeled check boxes. In their own way, each of these offers control over the environment in which your methods will run. The only one we really need at this level is **Var**.

2. Click on the **Var** check box to get a tick. While you are there, highlight the pushButton method. Click OK.

Variables 49

3. You should no have Edit windows open for both the Var and the pushButton method. Bring the Var editi window to the front. It will have a 'Var' header and an 'endVar' footer.

4. Edit it to read:

> **Var**
> **Choice   String**
> **endVar**

You now have somewhere in which you can store a string of text, and its name is Choice. You could have called it more or less anything you liked. The same rules apply here as for objects - any reasonable length and no spaces or punctuation. Nothing else is needed here. Run **Language|Check Syntax** to make sure there's no typing error and to save it.

5. Bring the pushButton window to the top. We'll use the new variable to store the value returned by the Yes/No/Cancel dialog box, and to control the program flow. Edit the existing method to give:

> **method pushButton(var eventInfo Event)**
> **msgInfo("Ouch","Not so hard!")**
> **Choice = msgYesNoCancel("Button Use","Will you be gentle next time?")**
> **if Choice = "No"**
> **   then msgInfo("Beast", "I shall sulk")**
> **   else if Choice = "Yes"**
> **then msgInfo("Thank You", "You are most kind.")**
> **   else msgInfo("Cancelling","You might reply.")**
> **   endif**
> **endif**
> **endmethod**

199

| 49 | Variables |

What's hapening here? The user's reply to the Yes/No/Cancel box is copied into Choice on the third line. If the output from the box is tested directly - as it was in the earlier version of this method - we can only test it once. But with the result stored in a variable, we can test that as often as we like. The test does not affect the variable in any way. Here we are running two **if** ... tests to produce suitable responses to "Yes" and "No" answers.

There are three possible outputs from a msgYesNoCancel() dialog box, and this method deals with them all.

A "No" response is picked up by the first test and gives the "Beast" message. If it is not "No", the method flows down the **else** branch to the second test, for "Yes". There is no explicit test for "Cancel", but it is not needed. If the response is neither "No" nor "Yes", the method will flow past the second **else** to get to the "Cancelling" message.

6. Check the syntax, return to View mode and test each of the three alternatives in turn.

To get a clearer idea of how the **if ... else ...** structure works, edit the method and remove first one, then the other **else**, testing between them. You should find that one can be removed without altering the final result, but that the other is crucial. Follow the logic to work out exactly what is happening.

Handling Files in Methods   50

The last examples have been short and trivial, but they should have illustrated some of the essentials of method-writing. This next example is equally short, but rather more useful. It demonstrates how to open and use files from a method. We are going to add a button to our Stock update form. When pressed, this will run the Reorder query and output the corresponding report.

Some commands are designed for use with specific types of files, and need only be supplied with a filename. e.g.

executeQBEfile("filename")

This opens and runs a predesigned query. As part of the built-in error trapping, this returns a TRUE value if the file was opened and run successfully. If the command cannot be executed, it returns a FALSE value. We can pick up the TRUE/FALSE value be enclosing the command in an **if ... then ... else ...** structure.

So, using the reorder query, this gives:

if executeQBEfile("reorder.qbe")
  then .... carry on
else ... report failure and stop

With other file commands, you must first set up a variable to hold temporary data for the file. This is the case when we want to open and print a report. The basic shape of that command is:

varname.open("filename")

Notice the punctuation in that line. In ObjectPAL commands that perform actions on objects are usually written in the form:

object.action(data)

201

50   Handling Files in Methods

Here the object is a variable of type Report - we'll call this 'stockRep' - and the data will be the name of the report file. The command line is then:

stockRep.open("reorder.rsl")

Having linked the filename "reorder.rsl" to the variable 'stockRep' when we opened the file, we do not need to give the filename in later operations. Thus, to print the report, we use the simpler:

stockRep.print()

Those brackets are still necessary after the command, even though there is no data in them.

Let's try and put this all together.

1. Open the Stock Update form that we created back in Section 31. Add a button to it, rename it 'ReorderList' and change the 'LABEL' to 'Reorder'. Open the button's Methods dialog box and tick the Var check box and highlight the pushButton method. Press OK and you'll have both editing windows open.

2. In the Var window, set up your Report variable:

Var
stockRep   Report
endVar

3. Edit the pushButton method as shown below.

202

Handling Files in Methods 50

```
method pushButton(var eventInfo Event)
   if executeQBEfile("reorder.qbe")
      then stockRep.open("reorder.rsl")
         stockRep.print()
         stockRep.close()
      else msgStop("Stop", "Failed to run query")
   endif
endmethod
```

This will attempt to run the query, and if successful, it will open, print and close the report. Notice those three commands are written on successive lines, with no special puctuation. When the method is executed, **if** the test proves true, every command from the **then** to the **else** will be performed.

If the query file cannot be found, the method branches to give a failure message. I've used a **msgStop()** dialog box here. This displays a message then ends the method. As it happens, the method would end in any case, so a **msgInfo()** would have done just as well.

Obviously, this will only work if you have the query "reorder.qbe" and the report "reorder.rsl", both based on that same Stock table. Browse the files or open the Folder to check that you are using the right names for your query and report files.

4. When you think you've got it typed in correctly, run **Check Syntax** to make sure. Any errors are most likely to be in the punctuation.

You can test this without actually sending the report to a printer. Before the file is output, the system will display the usual **Print the File** dialog box, which has a Cancel button. Cancelling the output

203

50   Handling Files in Methods

does not affect the method, which will carry on and close the file, whether it has been printed or not.

Does it work? Does it make life easier? Is it worth going a little deeper into methods? I trust you replied "Yes" three times.

Menus in Methods   51

Buttons are an excellent way to automate single actions, but are less convenient where you want to offer a set of options. True, you could create a button for each option, but there is a neater solution - the menu. ObjectPAL has all the objects and routines that you need to set up the same kind of menu system that is used by Paradox and other Windows applications. You can create a menu bar of options, with or without attached pop-up menus - which can themselves have pop-up menus linked to their options. Selection from the menus is by point and click or by initial letter, as is normal in Windows.

As elsewhere in ObjectPAL, all the hard work is done for you. The system knows what a menu is and what to do with it. To set one up, all you have to do is supply the names for the options. To use one to control the program flow, all that is needed is a variable to collect the value returned by the menu, then a set of **if ...** lines (or a **switch** structure - see below) to branch off to the routines for the different options.

We'll start with a trivial example to demonstrate the key points. The methods on this form will produce a simple menu bar with two options, one of which has a pop-up menu. Selections from this menu will display "Hello" and "Goodbye" messages. Apart from the menus themselves, there is nothing else new here.

1. Open a new blank form - not linked to any data model.

2. Get the Methods dialog box for the underlying page of the form - just click anywhere on the form.

3. Tick the **Var** box and click OK to open the **Var** window. The variables will be defined on the page itself, so that they are accessible to any method in the form.

205

51 Menus in Methods

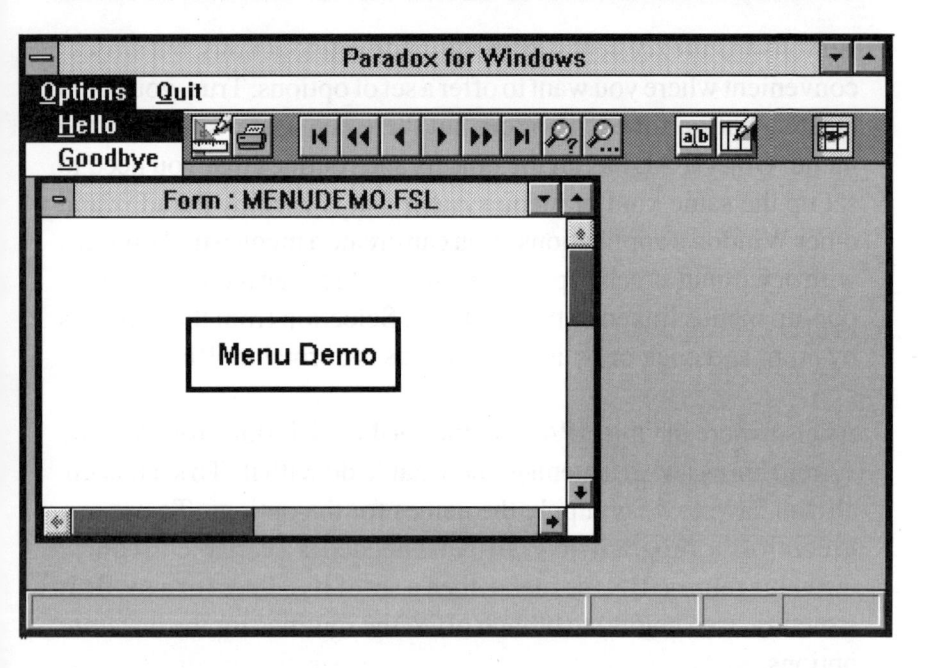

4. Our first job is to create the variables that will hold the menu data and the user's choice. There are two new types here - **Menu** and **PopUpMenu**. Their nature should be obvious. Change the variable names if you like - but take care to carry the new names through to the later methods. Your Var method should read:

```
Var
topMenu  Menu
pop      PopUpMenu
choice   String
endVar
```

The next job is to create the menus and get them on screen. The top bar will hold the words "Options" and "Quit". "Options" will then have a pop-up menu offering "Hello" and "Goodbye". There are three new commands here.

Menus in Methods   51

addText

Use this to write words into either a pop-up or a top bar menu. It follows the normal pattern of object.action(data).

pop.addText("&Hello")

This creates the label "Hello" in the menu called pop. Note the ampersand (&) before the "H". This makes "H" the active letter for keypress selection (the one that is underlined on the screen.) All menu words must have an ampersand before one letter - not necessarily the first. And, of course, you can't use the same selection letter twice in a menu. So, if you had "Query" and "Quit" in a set of options, you would want method lines like this:

myMenu.addText("&Query")   "Q" is the selector
myMenu.addText("Qui&t")   "T" is the selector

addPopUp

This adds a pop-up menu into a menu bar. The command needs two items of data, the header label - again with an ampersand before the selection letter, and the name of the po-up menu variable. Here, that gives us:

topMenu.addPopUp("&Options",pop)

show

After you have written your last 'addText' and 'addPopUp' to create the menu structure, use **show** to bring it onto the screen. It's a simple **object.action()** command, requiring no data.

207

51   Menus in Methods

The open Method

If you want the menu to appear automatically when the form is opened, as we do here, it should be written into the **open** method.

5. Get the Methods dialog box for your form, select **open** from the Built-in Methods and click OK.

6. Type in the command lines given below and check the syntax.

> **method open(var eventInfo Event)**
> **pop.addText("&Hello")**
> **pop.addText("&Goodbye")**
> **topMenu.addPopUp("&Options",pop)**
> **topMenu.addText("&Quit")**
> **topMenu.show()**
> **endmethod**

Don't try to run it yet. We still haven't written the method to handle the menu selections.

Handling Menu Selections   52

One of the built-in methods is **menuAction**. This picks up the mouse of keypress selection, returning the value through the expression **eventInfo.menuChoice()**. It's worth spending a moment looking at what that means.

In the top line of this method you will see the words **(var eventInfo MenuEvent)**. This sets up a variable of the right type to collect the mouse click or keypress of a menu selection. The action command **menuChoice()** returns the selection in the form of a menu label - i.e. "&Quit". We can transfer this to a simple String variable for later use in the method. Hence the line:

choice = eventInfo.menuChoice.

In this example, we are handling the menu selection in much the same way as we did the response from the Yes/No/Cancel dialog box earlier. A series of **if ...** statements, test the choice to see which label has been selected and to display suitable messages. Notice that the labels are written exactly the same as they were in the menus - complete with ampersands. This is important. The syntax checker won't complain if you miss the ampersands out, but the **if ...** tests will fail when you run the method.

Here's the basic method. Vary the messages to suit yourself. When it's typed in and checked, save the whole form, then take it for a test run. As the method is triggered by the opening of the form it will run automatically when you load it in, or - as now - when you switch from Design to Edit mode. You cannot, however, start it up from the form itself - as you could with a button. If you want to run it a second time, switch into Design mode and back out again.

You may then like to adapt the whole structure, adding more and different menu selections. Add a new pop-up menu, following the

209

52   Handling Menu Selections

pattern of the one given here. If you hit problems, get the Var, open and menuAction methods open on screen together and cross check the variable names and the menu text.

Note that the indents serve no special Paradox purpose. They are there so that you and I can see the structure more clearly. Make full use of tab indents, spaces and blank lines to produce more readable methods. Paradox will ignore them all quite happily.

```
method menuAction(var eventInfo MenuEvent)
choice = eventInfo.menuChoice()
if choice = "&Hello"
   then msgInfo("Hi","Hello")
endif
if choice = "&Goodbye"
   then msgInfo("Bye","Goodbye")
endif
if choice = "&Quit"
   then removeMenu()
endif
endmethod
```

That **removeMenu()** in the Quit option is an essential part of any menu-driven method. You must make sure that **removeMenu()** is performed before leaving the method. If it isn't, then the method's menu will stay in the top line of your Desktop in place of the normal Paradox one. You can get rid of it and restore normal operation by closing down the form that contains the offending method - but you have to know that. As the main point of methods is to make life easier, any method which leaves its users in the lurch is not a good method.

Handling Menu Selections 52

The switch structure

Where a program can branch off in any one of many different directions, the **switch** structure offers a more convenient alternative to a long set of if ... statements.

In essence, you have a series of tests - not necessarily on the same variable - each followed by one or more actions to be performed if the test is true. The start of each test and action set is marked by the word **case**. The special test word **otherwise** handles any inputs not catered for by the specific case tests. (This is optional, and omitting it has little effect in most cases.) The whole is enclosed by **switch** at the start and **endSwitch** after the last. That gives us the basic shape:

```
switch
   case (testOne)        : actionOne
   case (testTwo)        : actionTwoAlpha
                           actionTwoBeta
   case (testThree)      : actionThree
   otherwise             : defaultAction
endSwitch
```

To test this out, edit your menuAction method as shown here.

```
method menuAction(var eventInfo MenuEvent)
choice = eventInfo.menuChoice()
switch
   case choice = "&Hello"    : msgInfo("Hi","Hello")
   case choice = "&Goodbye"  : msgInfo("Bye","Goodbye")
   case choice = "&Quit"     : removeMenu()
   otherwise                 : enableDefault
endswitch
endmethod
```

211

52   Handling Menu Selections

In the last line you will see the command **enableDefault**. This triggers one of the system's built-in default routines. it is essential. Miss it out at your peril, for without it the whole Windows menu system can become corrupted!

Automated Stock Control

In these last two sections, the aim is to develop a set of ObjectPAL methods that will draw together the existing forms, queries and reports to produce a user-friendly menu-driven system. In the process we'll create some simple **custom** methods - these are ones that you write from scratch. That's not difficult here, where the methods that we are going to write will simply run queries and print reports.

If anything, the hardest part - certainly the part that requires the clearest thought - is planning the whole system. That task is easier where you already have the system running in 'manual' mode, i.e. all the forms, queries and reports exist but are controlled direct from the normal Paradox menus. That is the case here, and it's generally the best way to develop any system.

First check that all the components work properly and then observe your own actions carefully, until you are clear about what methods are needed and what they should do. If you can describe the operations in terms of the tasks to be performed and the files that will be used, then you are half way to writing the methods that will link them all together

1. File View / Update routines

    A. Major changes, requiring access to all fields.
       Task - open main form "STOCK.FSL".
       User to put in Edit mode if wanted.

    B. Stock Update & Availability check.
       Task - open limited form "STOCKUP.FSL".
       User to put in Edit mode if wanted.

53   Automated Stock Control

2. Reports

   A. Reorder levels
      Run query "REORDER.QBE".
      Open and print report "REORDER.RSL".

   B. Valuation
      Run query "VALUE.QBE".
      Open and print report "VALUE.RSL".

   C. Catalogue
      Run query "CATALOG.QBE".
      Open and print report "CATALOG.RSL"

If we arrange the method summaries by the tasks that they perform, we can see a possible menu structure.

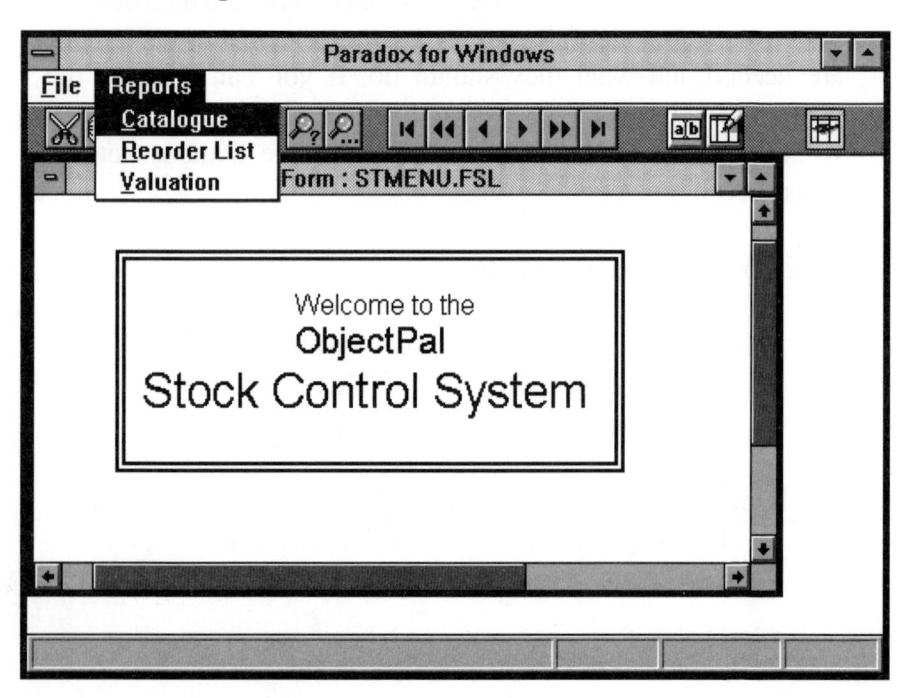

Automated Stock Control		**53**

Top Menu	File	Reports
Pop Ups	Main	Reorder
	Update	Valuation
	Quit	Catalogue

And with the menu and file objects known, we can list the types of variables that we will need. There will be some for the files, but as there will only be one form, query or report open at any one time, one of each type will do. We shall also want variables for the top and pop-up menus and a string to hold the menu selection.

Time to start writing the methods. You should work from the bottom upwards. If a method *calls* - i.e. sets in motion - another method, then you will get syntax errors if the subordinate one has not already been written and saved to the form. The same applies to variables. Where they are defined in the Var window, rather than in the methods which actually use them, you should set the Var up first.

1. Open a new form, without selecting a data model, so that it is blank. Open the Var window and create this set of variables:

    Var
        stockForm   **Form**
        stockQbe   **Query**
        stockRep   **Report**
        topMenu   **Menu**
        pop1,pop2   **PopUpMenu**
        choice   **String**
    endVar

2. Reopen the form's method box and select the **open** built-in method. This is where the menu system must be written if it is to

215

53   Automated Stock Control

be active automatically when the form is opened. Add the text to the two pop-up menus, add those to the main menu then set it to display. Your method should look like this:

method open(var eventInfo Event)
pop1.addText("&Main File")
pop1.addText("&Update")
pop1.addText("&Quit")
topMenu.addPopUp("&File",pop1)
pop2.addText("&Catalogue")
pop2.addText("&Reorder List")
pop2.addText("&Valuation")
topMenu.addPopUp("Reports",pop2)
topMenu.show()
endmethod

The menu selections will be handled by a **menuAction()** method, with branching run through a **switch** structure.

method menuAction(var eventInfo MenuEvent)
choice = eventInfo.menuChoice()
switch
   ...

This is much the same as we've done before. It's what happens next that is different. Some of the actions consist of single statements, and could be conveniently accommodated within the switch lines. e.g.

case choice = "&Main File" : stockForm.open("Stock.fsl")

Others consist of a series of statements. You can have multiple lines after a **case** test, just as you can after **then** or **else** of an **if ... then ... else ...** structure. This is valid:

216

Automated Stock Control

```
case choice = "&Reorder List":
  if executeQBEfile("reorder.qbe")
  then stockRep.open("reorder.rsl")
      stockRep.print()
  else msgStop("Stop", "Failed to run query")
  endif
case choice = ....
```

But it's not very elegant. A better solution is to make that block of code into a separate, **custom** method. This will allow you to keep the switch structure simple and easy to read - and therefore easier to extend or correct later. As a general rule, you will find it easier to work with a linked set of simple methods rather than one complex one. So, let's see how to create custom methods.

54   Custom Methods

Essentially, a custom method consists of one or more ObjectPAL statements, with an identifying header line and a closing 'endmethod' key word. The main difference between custom and built-in methods is that the latter are all linked to some event or other - opening a form, pressing a button, moving the mouse or whatever. Custom methods have no such linkage, and will be executed when they are activated from within another method.

To set up a new one, open the methods dialog box, click on the **New Custom Method** line to get the editing cursor and type in a suitable name. The rules for these are the same as for variables - don't use spaces or punctuation signs and, for your own benefit, make it brief but meaningful.

If, by any chance, you should hit on a name that has already been allocated to a built-in method, the system will assume that you really wanted that built-in one. You won't realise that it has done this until the next time that you open the methods dialog box, when you will see it listed with the built-ins, not the custom methods. Don't worry overmuch - it's very unlikely.

When the edit window opens for your new method, you will find that the header and footer lines have been written in for you. The header will include the name that you have given the method. So, if you wanted a method to handle the re-order report and had, quite reasonably, called it "reorder", you would now see:

method reorder()

endmethod

Those brackets after the name are where you would write in variables if you wanted to pass data to or from this method. They are

Custom Methods 54

not used in any of the following methods.

The code in this method is exactly the same as for the pushButton method in Section 50. It attempts to run the appropriate query, and if successful opens, prints and closes the reorder report.

```
method reorder()
if executeQBEfile("reorder.qbe")
  then stockRep.open("reorder.rsl")
       stockRep.print()
       stockRep.close()
else msgStop("Stop", "Failed to run query")
endif
endmethod
```

Type it in. Check the syntax and correct any errors. When it's right, go back to the methods dialog box and start on the next custom method - the one to produce the valuation report. Leave this editing window open! We can use it to speed up the writing of the next.

Shortcuts with Edit

Paradox offers the same cut-and-paste facilities that you find in all Windows applications. These can be very handy when writing methods, where you may well be using virtually the same piece of code on several occasions. That is the case here. The methods to produce the valuation and catalogue reports are identical to that for the reorder report, except for the filenames.

You should have open on your desktop the editing windows for the new valuation and the existing reorder methods. Bring the reorder one to the top.

54 Custom Methods

1. Click on the start of the text, beneath the header line. This will locate the editing cursor. Hold the left button down and drag the highlight over to the last line of the code you want to copy.

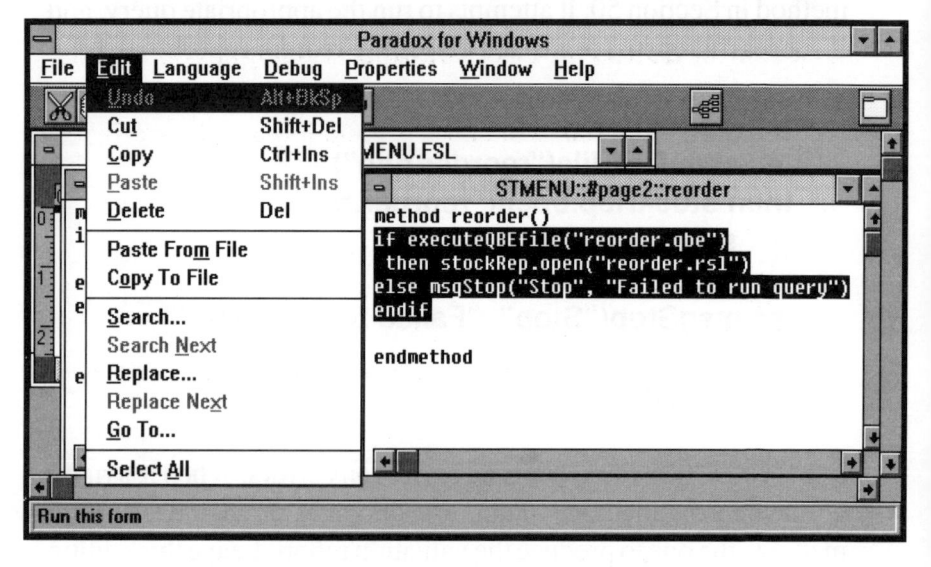

```
method reorder()
if executeQBEfile("reorder.qbe")
    then stockRep.open("reorder.rsl")
    else msgStop("Stop", "Failed to run query")
endif

endmethod
```

2. Pull down the **Edit** menu and select **Copy**. The lines have been saved in the Windows Clipboard.

3. Bring the new valuation method to the top. Click on the blank line beneath the header to locate the cursor.

4. Pull down the **Edit** menu again and select **Paste**. This should place a copy of the reorder code in the method.

5. Back to the **Edit** menu for one last job. You want to replace the two "reorder..." filenames with "value..." filenames. The search and replace facility will do this for you in one move.

Custom Methods 54

6. First locate the cursor somewhere above the first occurence of the word you want to replace - or after the last occurence. (The routine will work either up or down through the text.)

7. From the **Edit** menu select **Replace**. A dialog box opens. Click on the **Search** line and type "reorder". Do not press [Enter]! If you do, the routine will shoot off and replace the word with nothing - i.e. it will erase it.

8. Move to the **Replace** line, either with [Tab] or the mouse, and type in "value". Tick the Select All checkbox. If you left the cursor at the end of the text in the method, you should also select Up, to make the routine go backwards through the text. Press OK to run it.

221

54 Custom Methods

Your new method should look like this:

method valuation()
if executeQBEfile("value.qbe")
** then stockRep.open("value.rsl")**
**   stockRep.print()**
**   stockRep.close()**
else msgStop("Error", "Failed to run Query")
endif
endmethod

In exactly the same way, set up a new custom method for the catalogue report, using the edit facilities to create this:

method catalogue()
if executeQBEfile("catalog.qbe")
** then stockRep.open("catalog.rsl")**
**   stockRep.print()**
**   stockRep.close()**
else msgStop("Error", "Failed to run query")
endif
endmethod

The last three custom methods that you will need are shown here. **openMain()** and **update()** are so short that it seems scarcely worth the effort of making them into methods. Those single statements could quite easily fit into the switch structure of your menuAction method. The main reason for separating them off as methods is that it will simplify improvements. You might want to add error-checking or confirmation routines now, and perhaps later extend the automation, to make the updating routines more user-friendly and foolproof.

Custom Methods   54

```
method quitSystem()
if msgYesNoCancel("Quit", "Really exit?") = "Yes"
   then removeMenu()
endif
endmethod

method openMain()
stockForm.open("Stock.fsl")
endmethod

method update()
stockForm.open("Stockup.fsl")
endmethod
```

With the methods all written, checked and saved, you can write the menuAction method to tie them all together. It follows the same pattern as our earlier menu selection, but with the choices leading to methods rather than statements.

```
method menuAction(var eventInfo MenuEvent)
choice = eventInfo.menuChoice()
switch
   case choice = "&Main File"      :openMain()
   case choice = "&Update"         :update()
   case choice = "&Quit"           :quitSystem()
   case choice = "&Catalogue"      :catalogue()
   case choice = "&Reorder List"   :reorder()
   case choice = "&Valuation"      :valuation()
   otherwise                       :enableDefault
endSwitch
endmethod
```

223

| 54 | Custom Methods |

Good luck with it. I found the process of designing and writing this system fascinating, in that so much could be done with so little. I hope that you have also enjoyed the process and that you have been stimulated to take your ObjectPAL programming further.

Index

A

Add Band, in Reports 116
addPopUp, in Methods 207
addText, in Methods 207
Alias 36
Alias Manager 39
Alignment of Text, in Reports 119
Alphanumeric Field Type 20
AND operator 91
Answer Table in PRIV 82
Answer Table Properties 96
AS operator, in Queries 147

B

Band depth, adjusting 114
Bands, in Reports 113
Binary Field Type 22
BLOBs 22
Box, creating 70
Browser 37
Built-in Methods 191
Button tool 190

C

CALC 144
Calculated Fields, and Text 127
Calculated Fields, in Queries 144
Calculated Fields, in Reports 150
Case Sensitive, in searches 81
Categories, in Crosstabs 170
Contain Objects, Box Property 78
Create Table window 47
Crosstab, Defining 166
Currency Field Type 21

Index

D

Data	14
Data Entry, on Forms	67
Data Model dialog box	108
Data Type, in Graphs	173
Database Design	42
Database, Flat-file	18
Database Management System	18
Database, Relational	19
Date Field Type	21
Dates, in Queries	89
dBase File Formats	20
Default Field Values	50
Define Crosstab dialog box	167
Define Field dialog box	128
Define Graph dialog box	172
Define Group dialog box	116
Define List dialog box	138
Design mode, Forms	68
Design Objects	30
Design Preferences, Properties	111
Design Speedbar	112
Design Tools, in Forms	70
Desktop	26
Display Type, Property	75
Display Types, in Forms	136
Driver Type	40
Dropdown Edit, Display Type	137
DTP and restraint	121

E

Edit Data	57
Edit mode	56
Editing Methods	219
enableDefault, in Methods	212
Events	188

Index

Exact Match, in searches 81
Exact Matches, in Queries 86
Examples, in Queries 139
executeQBEfile, in Methods 201
Expanded Ruler 118

F

Field 16
Field Properties 75
Field Roster 48
Field, Selection in Reports 109
Field Selection Modes, in Queries 84
Field Structure 31
Field Structure, Design 44
Field View, for editing 58
Field View, Key Controls 59
Field Widths, Changing 63
Fields, Moving 63
File 17
File Formats 20
File menu 27
File|New|Form 68
File|New|Query 83
File|New|Report 108
File|New|Table 47
File|Open 54
File|Save 52
Filenames, Rules 52
Flat-file Database 18
Folder 29
Folder|Add Item 131
Folder|Remove Item 131
Font, Text Property 78
Form 32
Form design 136
Form|Design 68
Form|Edit Data 67, 72

227

Index

Form|End Edit 67
Format of Answer Table 97
Formatted Memo Field Type 22
Forms, Key Controls 67
Forms, Movement 66
Forms, selecting objects 69
Formulae for Calculated Fields 151

G

GIGO 15
Graph Properties 173
Graph Types, variety of 178
Graphic Field Type 22
Graphic File Formats 158
Graphics in Forms 162
Graphics in Reports 158
Graphics in Tables 161

I

if ... then ... endif, in Methods 196
if command, in Methods 195
Image, in Query Editor 83
Indents, in Report Text 119
Information 14

J

Just Selected, Sort option 98

K

Key Field 18
Key Fields, Defining 48
Key violation 135

L

Labels 122
Legend, in Graphs 175
LIKE operator 87

228

Index

Line, drawing 70
Line Spacing, in Reports 119
List, Display Type 137
Locate 79
Locate Value dialog box 80

M

Magnification, of Graphics 160
Major Objects 30
Maximum Value, in Field 49
Memo Field Type 22
Menu Bar 27
Menu, in Methods 206
menuAction, in Methods 209
Methods, Built-In 191
Methods, Designing 213
Methods dialog box 191
Minimum Value, in Field 49
msgInfo, in Methods 192
msgStop, in Methods 203
msgYesNoCancel, in Methods 195
Multi-record 122
Multi-record, Report style 122

N

New Custom Method 218
Number Field Type 21
Number Formats 77

O

Object-Oriented Programming 188
Objects 30
Objects, Renaming 190
OLE Field Type 22
OOPS 188
Open Method 208
Open Project Folder 130

Index

Open Table Dialog Box 55
Opening Files 54
Opening Files in Methods 202
OR operator 91

P

Page band 113
Page Layout, for Reports 123
Paste From Graphic File 159
Picture Formats 50
PopUpMenu, in Methods 206
Print File dialog box 106
PRIV alias 36
Private Directory 39
Properties menu, Desktop 27
Properties of Fields 75
Properties of Objects 30,74
Properties|Answer Table 96
Properties|Define OLE 163
Properties|Designer 111
Properties|Display Type 136

Q

QBE 83
Query 34
Query By Example 139
Query, Defining 83
Query Editor window 83
Query|Add Table 141
Query|Run 85
Quick Form 65
Quick Graph 171
Quick Report 104

R

Radio Buttons, Display Type 137
Raster Operation options 160

230

Index

Record 16
Record band 113
Record, Deleting 60
Record menu 59
Record Selection in Queries 86
Record|Locate Value 79
Records, Moving between 59
Relational Database 19
Relational Operators 88
removeMenu, in Methods 210
Renaming Tables 95
Report 33
Report Design 111
Report|Print 105
Reports, designing 108
Required Field 49
Run Time Properties 76

S

Save Table As.. dialog box 52
Saving Files 52
Saving Queries 93
Script 35
Search & Replace, in Methods 221
Selecting Objects, in Forms 69
Series, in Graphs 174
Short Numbers Field Type 20
show, in Methods 207
Sort Order, setting 100
Sorting 98
Speed Bar 28
Status Bar 28, 29
Summaries, in Crosstabs 168
Summary Graphs 176
switch, in Methods 211
Syntax Checks, ObjectPAL 193
Syntax Errors 193

231

Index

T

Table	31
Table|End Edit	62
Table|Field View	58
Table|Quick Form	65
Table|Quick Graph	172
Table|Quick Report	104
Table|Rename	95
Table|Sort	98
Tabs, in Reports	119
Text, adding to Forms	71
Text, in Reports	118
Text tool, in Form Design	72

U

Update, OLE objects	164

V

Validity Checks	49
Var method	198
Variables, scope of	198
View Data, in Reports	112
View mode, Forms	66
View mode, Tables	56

W

Wildcards	81
Wildcards, in Queries	87
Window menu	28
Word Wrap, Property	75
WORK alias	36
Working Directory	36, 37